# RODALE ORGANIC GARDENING BASICS

# soil

RODALE

## From the Editors of
## Rodale Organic Gardening
## Magazine and Books

© 2000 by Rodale Inc.

The information in this book has been carefully researched, and all efforts have been made to ensure accuracy. Rodale Inc. assumes no responsibility for any injuries suffered or for damages or losses incurred during the use of or as a result of following this information. It is important to study all directions carefully before taking any action based on the information and advice presented in this book. When using any commercial product, *always* read and follow label directions. Where trade names are used, no discrimination is intended and no endorsement by Rodale Inc. is implied.

Printed in the United States of America on acid-free ∞, recycled ♻ paper

We're always happy to hear from you. For questions or comments concerning the editorial content of this book, please write to:

Rodale Book Readers' Service
33 East Minor Street
Emmaus, PA 18098

Look for other Rodale books wherever books are sold. Or call us at (800) 848-4735.

For more information about Rodale Organic Gardening magazine and books, visit us at:

www.organicgardening.com

Editors: Deborah L. Martin and Karen Costello Soltys
Contributing Editor: Christine Bucks
Interior Book Designer: Nancy Smola Biltcliff
Interior Illustrator: Anthony Davis
Cover Designer: Patricia Field
Photography Editor: Lauren Hicks Shelley
Layout Designer: Dale Mack
Researchers: Sarah Wolfgang Heffner, Pamela R. Ruch, and Heidi A. Stonehill
Copy Editors: Christine Bucher and Stacey Follin
Manufacturing Coordinator: Mark Krahforst
Indexer: Nan Badgett
Editorial Assistance: Kerrie A. Cadden and Celia Leigh Cameron

**RODALE ORGANIC GARDENING BOOKS**
Managing Editor: Fern Marshall Bradley
Executive Creative Director: Christin Gangi
Art Director: Patricia Field
Production Manager: Robert V. Anderson Jr.
Studio Manager: Leslie M. Keefe
Associate Copy Manager: Jennifer Hornsby
Manufacturing Manager: Mark Krahforst

**Library of Congress
  Cataloging-in-Publication Data**
  Rodale organic gardening basics. Soil / from the editors of Rodale Organic Gardening Magazine and Books.
        p.    cm.
    Includes bibliographical references and index.
    ISBN 0-87596-838-4 (pbk. : alk. paper)
    1. Garden soils.   2. Organic gardening.
  I. Rodale Books.
  S596.75 .075   2000
  635'.0489—dc21                    99–050443

Distributed in the book trade by St. Martin's Press

2  4  6  8  10  9  7  5  3       paperback

# contents

# Learning to Love Your Soil

Most people take soil for granted. To them, soil is the stuff that fills in the space between buildings and roads. Some people don't even *like* soil—especially when other people (you know who you are) track it into the house when they've just washed the floor.

Sometimes, people want to love their soil. They want to work with the soil and plant a beautiful garden. But the soil is so hard and difficult to work with that these people start to wonder whether their soil is out to get them!

Having good soil—fluffy, healthy, rich soil—can mean the difference between a great garden and an unsuccessful one. Good soil has tons of great stuff in it, including living things like earthworms, microbes, and yes, even bugs. The more living things in the soil, the better plants will grow.

Here's the good news: Great soil can be made. By you. For free. How?

Well, almost any plant material that comes from your yard can be returned to it to build the soil. Sound hard? It's not hard at all; it's as easy as making compost. In this book we'll show you how making compost and taking care of your soil will lead to your best garden ever.

All without toxic chemicals, of course. And that's important for you and your family—and for those living things in the soil, which chemical fertilizers and pesticides can kill.

So read on to find out everything *you* need to know about the care and feeding of great soil.

Happy organic gardening!

*Maria Rodale*

Maria Rodale

> **The more living things in the soil, the better plants will grow.**

Plants get everything they need to thrive from the soil, including nutrients, water, and air.

# chapter one

# Healthy Soil, Healthy Plants

Want a great garden? A lush lawn? A beautiful border? Before you spend a dime on seeds, sod, or plants, start with the soil. Because if your soil isn't up to snuff, your plants don't stand a chance, no matter how much money you spend, or how much time you invest.

## SOIL: IT'S MORE THAN JUST DIRT

The soil beneath your garden, your lawn, and your flowerbeds is more than just a gigantic container that holds whatever plants you stick into it. Soil is a complex combination of minerals, organic matter (such as leaves and plant roots), humus (decayed organic matter), water, air, microorganisms, and other animals. And almost everything that's in the soil is essential for growing plants. So stop treating soil like it's nothing more than dirt, and you'll enjoy gardening success beyond your wildest dreams.

**Stop treating soil like it's nothing more than dirt, and you'll enjoy gardening success beyond your wildest dreams.**

### What Soil Does for Plants

Sure, soil holds plants up and gives them a place to spread their roots. But that's just the beginning of a beautiful relationship that's more complex than anything you've seen on the afternoon soaps.

Except for sunlight, plants get everything they need to grow and thrive from the soil they grow in. So if you want to give your garden, your lawn, or your landscape a boost, start with the soil. Here's the scoop on what's in there:

**Fresh air.** Roots need air, and if your soil doesn't have spaces to hold air, your plants basically suffocate.

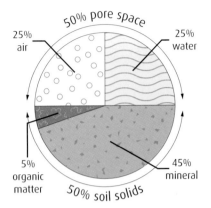

50% pore space

25% air

25% water

5% organic matter

45% mineral

50% soil solids

*The spaces in soil are just as important as the minerals and organic matter. Healthy soil has lots of tiny open spaces to hold the air, water, and nutrients that plants need to survive.*

## quick tip

While you're rethinking your views on soil, let's get rid of the d-word, too. Stop treating your soil like dirt, and stop calling it that. Dirt is what you get on your pants when you're retrieving the kids' ball from under the car. Soil is the foundation that nurtures and nourishes everything you grow. Give it the respect it deserves.

Adding organic matter, such as compost, to the soil helps to "fluff it up" so that there's room for air—and growing roots—between the soil particles.

**Moisture management.** Healthy soil holds water, too. Because plants like their nutrients in liquid form for easy absorption through their roots, water is essential for healthy plants. But too much water forces the air out of the soil and "drowns" your precious plants. Care for your soil, and it will handle this whole air-water balancing act for you.

**Good eats.** The nutrients that plants don't make for themselves through photosynthesis, they get from the soil. Healthy soil contains just the right mix of elements to support plant growth and development.

**All the right friends.** Earthworms, bacteria, fungi, insects, and all kinds of other critters inhabit healthy, organically tended soil. Far from harming your plants, these soil dwellers—big and small—help create spaces in the soil where roots can grow, break down organic matter into forms your plants can use, form connections with plant roots that improve nutrient uptake, and so much more.

## 5 THINGS YOU CAN STOP DOING NOW

Healthy soil forms the foundation for successful gardens, lawns, and landscapes. By building the soil, you create the best conditions for growing healthy, beautiful, productive plants. But caring for the soil sometimes means doing more by doing less. Organic soil care is as much about ending harmful practices as it is about adding to your list of gardening tasks. Read on to learn five things that you may be doing that are, at the least, unnecessary—and that may even be detrimental to your soil.

## 1. STOP Ignoring Your Soil!

If you expect your soil to support great gardens and a lush lawn year after year without any help from you, you're in for a disappointment. Organic matter is the stuff that all those helpful soil organisms use to nourish your plants and over time, it gets used up. If you don't replenish the soil's natural storehouse of nutrients by adding organic matter, eventually your plants will suffer.

And if you live in a newly built home, the surrounding surface soil may have been removed during construction and never properly restored. In this situation, there's no good way to make do with what's there—dig in and start adding organic matter as soon as possible.

## 2. STOP Using Chemical Fertilizers!

Feeding your plants with chemical (also called "synthetic") fertilizers gives you short-term gains in growth at the expense of long-term soil health. Because they're highly soluble, chemical fertilizers tend to wash through the soil quickly. If plants don't use them, they can end up as pollutants in groundwater. They're also harmful to earthworms and other soil organisms that work so hard at turning organic matter into humus and nutrients for your plants.

Instead, feed your plants with organic bagged fertilizers, or better still, feed your plants and soil compost you've made yourself. You'll save money and make your soil happy at the same time.

**quick tip**

One fast and easy step you can take to help your soil is to cover it up! Even if you don't plan to plant a garden right away, start improving the soil in your garden beds by covering it with a 1-inch-thick layer of organic mulch like shredded leaves, compost, or grass clippings.

*Never use chemical fertilizers. They may pollute groundwater and harm earthworms and other beneficial soil organisms.*

*If you want a lush-looking land-scape like this one, you need to stop ignoring your soil.*

### 3. STOP Compacting the Soil!

Repeatedly walking on soil or driving equipment such as a lawn tractor over soil compacts it, destroying the valuable spaces that hold air and water for your plants. To stop compacting your soil, vary the pattern you follow when you mow your lawn, and use stepping stones or a thick layer of mulch over paths to reduce compaction.

### 4. STOP Adding Lime (or Other Things) Just Because Your Neighbor Does!

Unless a soil test clearly indicates that there's something lacking in your soil, adding amendments or fertilizers is like burning piles of money in your yard. Worse, you may really throw things out of balance and wind up spending even more on amendments to correct the problems you've caused. To learn about how to test your soil, turn to "Getting Serious about Soil" on page 37.

# YOUR BIGGEST GRASS-ROOTS SUPPORTER

WHEN IT COMES TO SOIL CARE, most of us focus on the vegetable garden or on the border full of prized perennials. We amend and till; we fertilize and mulch and test. But we rarely give a thought to the biggest expanse of soil in the landscape—the soil that's supporting the lawn. Typically ignored and abused, the soil beneath your lawn is every bit as important as the pampered ground under the rosebush. Yet it suffers in silence while we compact it with foot traffic and heavy lawn mowers, and while we steal organic matter and nutrients by removing grass clippings. But a great-looking lawn depends on great soil underneath it. And years of ignoring that soil will result in a sparse, weedy, sickly lawn. Don't neglect your lawn! Here are three simple things you can do for your lawn's biggest grass-roots supporter:

- If your lawn needs help, start with a soil test. Add only the amendments indicated by the test results.

- Leave the clippings where they fall. If you've heard that this practice contributes to thatch buildup, forget this myth! Grass clippings add organic matter and nitrogen to the soil, improving its fertility, its structure, and its water-holding capacity. And they stimulate earthworm activity, which actually helps to break down thatch.

- Drop your rake and mow over your fallen leaves. By only raking the heavy accumulations, you can save time while building the soil under your lawn.

## 5. STOP Buying So Much Peat Moss!

Peat moss is a popular soil covering and soil amendment, but peat is a limited resource, and when used as a mulch, it can crust over and prevent moisture from penetrating your soil. Unless you're using peat to acidify the soil for plants such as blueberries or azaleas, save your money and substitute compost or shredded leaves.

*quick tip*

Peat moss in the soil is a lot like fiber in your diet: It helps hold water and nutrients and adds bulk. But peat itself contains few nurients, it's expensive, and it's very acidic. To make the most of your soil-building budget, save peat moss purchases for seed-starting or for amending the soil around acid-loving plants like rhododendrons.

## SUPPORT YOUR LOCAL SOIL

Healthy soil won't happen overnight, or even in one growing season. If you've relied on chemical fertilizers in the past, you may wonder if it's worth the long-term effort to build soil organic matter. But improving your soil organically will do more in the long run to reduce the amount you're spending on fertilizers. Healthy, balanced soil is easier to dig and plant in, requires less watering, and supports plants that are less susceptible to insect and disease problems. Follow these steps to build rich, healthy soil that your gardens will thrive in:

1. **Learn about your soil.** Test your soil (or have it tested at a lab) to find out about its structure, to find out how much organic matter and soil life it contains, and to find out what nutrients it holds for your plants. See "Getting to Know Your Soil" on page 9 for information on tests you can do yourself, or turn to "Soil-Care Secrets" on page 37 to learn about lab testing.

2. **Get your soil in balance.** Use soil amendments in recommended amounts to correct problems indicated by soil-test results. This process may take two to four years, depending on the condition of the soil when you start. Check out "Soil-Care Secrets" on page 37 for complete coverage of organic fertilizers and soil amendments.

*Take the time to improve your soil organically, and you'll have healthy soil that's easy to dig and plant in and that requires less watering.*

3. **Keep your balance**—your soil's balance, that is. Periodically adding materials to maintain soil organic matter is the key to keeping your soil healthy (in balance). A steady supply of organic matter feeds soil microorganisms and other soil dwellers, such as earthworms, which in turn help process the nutrients in organic matter into forms your plants can use.

4. **Feed your plants** (if you feel like it). Plants growing in balanced, healthy soil usually grow well without the need for additional fertilizer. Nourishing plants with additional organic fertilizer is an optional step when you decide the extra effort is worthwhile.

*Teeming with life, a handful of healthy soil holds a wealth of information about what your garden needs to succeed.*

chapter two

# Getting to Know Your Soil

Soil is wonderfully alive. If you're new to organic gardening, that statement may surprise you. But beneath the surface, healthy soil is full of organisms that interact in a finely tuned living system. Explore your soil. Learn about its texture and structure, and meet the tenants that live there, too. You'll find there's a lot that your soil and its inhabitants can do for your garden—with just a little help from you.

## DIG IN AND LEARN

Unless you're the lucky owner of an old farmstead, you probably don't have great soil in your yard and garden. The soil around most modern homes is in trouble, either because of damage during construction or neglect by past owners. But how do you decide what your soil really needs? What would benefit your plants most? And where do you begin?

Get to know your soil. Once you start digging around, you'll find there's more to it than meets the eye. Healthy soil has lots of life in it, a good balance of nutrients available for plants' use, and a loose, open structure. The way you manage and work the soil affects all these aspects of soil health. This chapter introduces some of the organisms you may meet when you take a closer look at your soil. It also explains how to do a few simple tests that can tell you a lot about what's happening in the soil beneath your gardens, lawn, and landscape.

Discover which soil critters are good ones and which ones are bad news. Learn about the structure, texture, drainage, and pH of the soil that surrounds your home. Equipped with this knowledge, you can

**Get to know your soil. Once you start digging around, you'll find there's more to it than meets the eye.**

begin to make smart choices about the soil-care techniques that make the most sense for you, your gardens, your lawn, and your landscape.

## THE GOOD GUYS IN THE GROUND

As you dig into your soil and become more familiar with its characteristics, you'll undoubtedly encounter some of the many insects and other creatures of

*Firefly*

all sizes that dwell in the soil's depths. Although they make up only a minute portion of the soil by weight and volume, these living organisms play a vital role in the soil's health. When you meet any of the soil-dwellers shown on this page (and one on the next), squelch your impulse to squash, and let them go safely about their business. These are just a few of the good guys who give gardeners a helping hand in exchange for their housing in the soil.

When you see **fireflies** (*Photuris* species)—commonly called "lightning bugs"—twinkling on a summer evening, be glad for their hungry, soil-dwelling larvae. Resembling sowbugs, firefly larvae prey on slugs, snails, cutworms, and mites. The larvae live in the soil for one to two years

*Fiery searcher*

before pupating inside a hard brown casing. Firefly adults emerge after about ten days and live for up to one week.

Many of the more than 3,000 species of ground beetles in North America prey on slugs, snails, cutworms, and caterpillars, but few are as voracious as the inch-long and extremely beneficial **fiery searcher** (*Calosoma scrutator*). Fiery searchers can live up to three years, and the adults will often climb trees in search of tent caterpillars to eat!

**Millipedes** (*Diplopoda* family) can range from ½ to 1½ inches long and move very slowly. Most feed only on decaying plants, breaking them down into organic matter for your soil. As predators, millipedes can eat many kinds of soil insects.

Millipede

## DOWN-'N-DIRTY SOIL DWELLERS

Of course, not every insect you turn up with your shovel is a beneficial. And it pays to recognize the bad guys when you run into them, if only because it gives you the option of tossing them out onto bare ground where a hungry bird can find them.

**Cabbage maggots** (*Delia radicum*) tunnel into the roots and stems of cabbage and related crops, causing wilting and generally poor productivity. The ¼-inch-long cabbage maggots can survive the winter as pupae in the upper layers of the soil; you can make them freeze to death by cultivating the soil in late winter to expose them to the air.

Cabbage maggot

**Symphylans** (*Scutigerella immaculata*) are pests that eat the roots of asparagus, cucumber, lettuce, radish, and tomato seedlings. Sometimes called "garden centipedes," symphylans resemble true centipedes but are only ¼ inch long with 12 pairs of legs. Fortunately, symphylan populations rarely reach damaging levels. True centipedes are larger and darker with 15 or more pairs of legs and are beneficials that prey on pest insects and mites.

Symphylan (close-up view)

The **June** or **May beetle grub** (*Phyllophaga* species) feeds on the roots of strawberries and potatoes during the spring and summer and can grow as big as 1 inch long. The grubs may remain in the ground for two years or more before emerging.

There are many different kinds of cutworms, but perhaps the most troublesome and widespread in North America is the **army cutworm** (*Euxoa auxiliaris*).

June beetle grub

At over 1 inch in length, cutworms are hefty opponents for gardeners trying to protect young plants. The cutworms feed just below the soil surface (or just above it), severing the stems of seedlings and transplants. Dig in the soil around the base of an injured plant and you're likely to find this culprit.

# UNSEEN SOIL OCCUPANTS

SOIL CONTAINS many organisms that you can't see (unless you look at a crumb of your soil through a microscope). Perhaps most mysterious—at least to gardeners—among the microscopic masses of protozoa, bacteria, and fungi are the nematodes. Also called threadworms or eelworms, nematodes are slender, translucent, wormlike organisms. Some nematodes are large enough to be seen with the naked eye, but most are microscopic.

Most nematodes are good guys, parasitizing pests such as root weevils, crown and stem borers, corn rootworms, and potato maggots. They're so effective that farmers sometimes buy parasitic nematodes in large quantities and apply them to their fields to control pests. Other nematodes are like miniature earthworms—only about ¼ inch long—that help break down organic matter in the soil.

The relatively few species of pest nematodes have given a bad name to the many beneficial nematodes that live in the soil. The infamous pest nematodes can cause root knots or galls, injured root tips, and distorted leaves on everything from vegetable crops to peonies. But it takes a lot of these tiny pests to cause serious plant injury, and several years for a nematode population to build to a damaging level.

If you suspect that you have pest nematodes in your soil, consult your local cooperative extension office to confirm that nematodes are the cause of your troubles. You can prevent nematode problems by rotating garden crops from one year to the next. Or solarize your soil to rid it of existing pest nematodes. Solarization involves covering moist soil with clear plastic during the summer months, heating the soil enough to kill the pest nematodes in it.

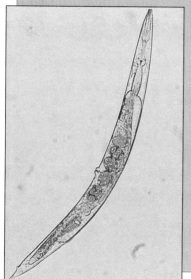

*Nematode (as seen through microscope)*

Down where your root crops live, you'll find the ½-inch-long adult **carrot beetle** (*Bothynus ligyrus*), which feeds on the stems and roots of beets, carrots, parsnips, and potatoes.

The small—only ¼ inch long—**subterranean termite** (*Reticulitermes* species) eats the decaying roots of plants and trees and builds tunnels in wood, which can include your house.

*Cutworm*

**Northern mole crickets** (*Neocurtilla hexadactyla*) are mostly destructive, chewing up the roots of crops, eating seeds, and severing the stems of tender transplants. But these 1- to 1½-inch-long crickets also eat other insects.

**Colorado potato beetle** (*Leptinotarsa decemlineata*) adults and grubs feed on the leaves of potatoes, eggplant, and related crops and spend their winters underground. The adults are ⅓ to ½ inch long, and the grubs are somewhat smaller.

*Carrot beetle*

Lawns are the favorite feeding ground for the grubs of the **Japanese beetle** (*Popillia japonica*), so you're most likely to see the ¾-inch grubs when you turn over sod for new garden plots. Treating your lawn with milky disease spores is a safe, long-term control for these pests.

*Subterranean termites*

*Colorado potato beetle grub*

*Japanese beetle grub*

*Colorado potato beetle adult*

*Northern mole cricket*

TO GET AN ESTIMATE of the earthworm population in your soil, dig a hole 8 to 10 inches deep and a foot wide and count the number of earthworms you find in the soil you remove. More than ten earthworms is great, and six to ten indicates a moderately healthy soil, but if you have less than five you need to do some serious work on the soil! This could be an indication of low organic matter, pH problems, and/or poor drainage.

If your earthworm count is low, don't despair. Once you provide more organic material to feed them, they will return. Healthy soil can contain about 1.5 million worms per acre—even more reason not to underestimate the importance of these ambitious decomposers. And if you think that number sounds surprisingly high, consider that worms multiply extremely quickly—producing upward of 2,000 to 3,000 offspring per worm per year.

# THE WONDER OF WORMS

It's easy to take earthworms for granted because they work out of sight, deep within the soil. But in a year, an acre of worms can move 20 tons of earth. Simply by tunneling through the soil, worms break up compacted earth so that air and water can circulate more freely. They chow down on dead leaves, bits of soil, rotting plants, and other nourishing debris (collectively called organic matter), grinding the material in their gizzards. What comes out the other end is a magical elixir that increases the amount of nutrients and minerals in the soil by as much as ten times the value of the plant debris there.

Worm droppings, known as "castings," are the richest food your plants' roots will ever find. Worm action also creates great texture in soil. As the worms turn raw organic material into humus, the soil becomes moist, loose, and more like the ideal loam plants love. If your soil is healthy, it will be full of earthworms.

*Curious youngsters and hungry robins may pluck a few earthworms from your garden, but don't worry about the worms. Keep feeding the soil with organic matter and there'll be plenty of worms for all.*

## HANDS-ON TEXTURE TESTS

Pick up a handful of soil. Is it gritty? Sticky? Smooth or greasy? How your soil feels when you hold it in your hand is a function of its texture. Texture refers to the relative amounts of the different-size mineral particles in the soil. Clay particles are the smallest, silt particles are somewhat larger, and sand particles are the biggest.

But these different types of particles do more than make the soil feel a certain way when you stick your toes into it. The size of the particles determines how tightly they bind together and, therefore, how much space there is in the soil for air and water—and for growing roots.

Learning what texture your soil has is as easy as picking up a handful of soil and squeezing it. Start with this simple test: When the earth is moist but not wet, take a loose ball of soil about the size of a golf ball in the palm of your hand. First, squeeze the ball in your hand and release. If it crumbles, it has a reasonably balanced texture. If the soil ball holds its shape, it has a substantial percentage of clay.

*Squeezing a handful of soil into a ball (left) and pressing it out into a ribbon shape (right) are two easy tests that can tell you how much clay is in your soil.*

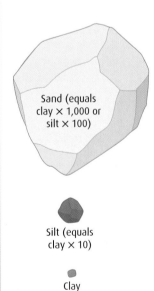

Sand (equals clay × 1,000 or silt × 100)

Silt (equals clay × 10)

Clay

*The size of the particles in your soil determines how much space there is for air and water.*

Good soil drainage prevents plant disease problems: Because most fungi germinate in moist to wet conditions, good soil drainage is crucial to preventing disease problems. When you garden organically, you'll find that your soil drainage is bound to improve, because you'll be adding organic matter to your soil on a regular basis. So you'll be fighting disease problems without even trying!

Another hands-on texture test is called the "ribbon" test. Holding the soil in the palm of your hand, squeeze gently so it starts to come out between your thumb and forefinger. Use your thumb to press the soil out into a ribbon shape over the side of your finger. The longer the ribbon of soil, the more clay content your soil has. If the soil is too crumbly to form a ribbon, it has a good balance of sand, silt, and clay particles in it.

### READING YOUR RIBBONS

*Sandy loams and silty loams are light-textured soils. Silty clay and clay are heavy-textured soils. Everything else can be categorized as medium texture.*

| Ribbon Length | Feels Mostly Gritty | Feels Mostly Smooth | Feels Both Gritty and Smooth |
|---|---|---|---|
| Shorter than 1" | Sandy loam | Silty loam | Loam |
| 1"–2" long | Sandy clay loam | Silty clay loam | Clay loam |
| Longer than 2" | Sandy clay | Silty clay | Clay |

From *Start with the Soil*

## SOIL TEXTURE TEST IN A JAR

To get an even clearer picture of the relative amounts of clay, silt, and sand in your soil, try this easy technique for separating the different sizes of particles. You'll need a clear glass jar with a lid; water; 1 cup of dry, finely crumbled soil; 1 teaspoon of nonsudsing dishwasher detergent; and a crayon. To get a soil sample that's representative of your entire garden, take little samples from various places in your garden.

**1.** Fill the jar two-thirds full of water, add the soil and detergent, fasten the lid, and shake the jar for one minute. Place the jar on a level surface.

**2.** Sand particles will settle to the bottom first. After a minute passes, mark the sand level with the crayon.

*Mixing a soil sample in water and noting how the different sizes of soil particles settle into layers reveals the relative amounts of sand, silt, and clay in your soil.*

**3.** After two hours, mark the level of silt (the next layer of sediment that appears) on the jar.

**4.** After a few days, mark the third layer that forms, which is the clay.

If one type of particle makes up more than half of the total amount of soil in the jar, that is your dominant soil type. If the three layers are relatively equal, your soil is probably loamy—the best type of soil texture for growing plants.

## WET OR DRY?

How quickly—or how slowly—water travels through your soil is an important factor in determining which plants you can grow in your garden and in your landscape. As with most soil conditions, moderation is ideal. Very dry soil is no more desirable than very wet soil, although there are ways to solve both situations.

With a shovel, a watch, and your garden hose or a big bucket of water, you can get a reasonably clear picture of how well your soil drains. Dig a hole 6 to 12 inches deep and 6 to 12 inches wide. Fill the hole with water and let it drain. Soil with good drainage should absorb the water in 15 to 30 minutes. If the water drains faster than that, your soil doesn't hold water well and probably has a lot of sand in it. If it drains more slowly, your soil has poor structure and/or a lack of pore spaces between soil particles—it probably has a lot of clay in it. Either situation makes it harder to get plants to grow successfully without improving the soil.

*Timing how quickly water drains from a hole you've dug is an easy way to test your soil's drainage. A hole that's 6 to 12 inches deep and wide should empty within 15 to 30 minutes.*

## PH, WEEDS, AND OTHER SOIL HEALTH INDICATORS

Sweet or sour? Acid or alkaline? Gardeners use terms like these to describe soil pH—the measure of its acidity or alkalinity. Gardeners care about soil pH because it affects whether plants can take up the nutrients in the soil through their roots. Although some of your plants may have specific pH preferences, most will tolerate a fairly wide range of soil pH. To find out your soil's pH, you can have a sample tested by a laboratory, or buy a simple home pH test kit and do it yourself.

A pH reading of less than 6.0 indicates that your soil is too acidic—or sour—for most plants to thrive in. To raise the pH, spread ground limestone on your soil and work it into the top few inches. A pH level above 7.0 means that your soil is alkaline, or sweet. Sulfur is the amendment most often used to lower soil pH. Another way to help adjust your pH is by regularly adding organic matter over time. The organic matter will eventually help to balance the nutrients in the soil and bring the pH into the optimal range for plant growth of 6.2 to 7.0. For more information on pH and how to adjust your soil's pH, see "The Ups and Downs of Ph" on page 42.

## CAN THIS SOIL BE SAVED?

POOR DRAINAGE, a common condition in soils with a high clay content, can give your plants a bad case of "wet feet," or soggy soil around the roots. Because sodden soil spells trouble for many garden and landscape plants, gardeners with wet sites are faced with two options: Amend the soil or change the plants.

If you'd rather not invest your time and energy in modifying a perpetually soggy spot, create a garden that will thrive in the extra moisture. Plants such as ornamental willows, shrub dogwoods, Japanese iris, primroses, and cardinal flower all grow very nicely in swampy soil.

If you do want to improve your soil's drainage, you can add sand. The only problem with this approach is that it takes a lot of sand (at least a 1-to-2-inch-thick layer over the entire area you're amending) to counteract the poor drainage of clay. Also, sand doesn't do much to improve anything other than drainage, and it's not likely to encourage earthworms to help with your problem site. To truly improve a damp-soil location, plan to work in plenty of organic matter—at least a 1-inch-thick layer each year—along with ample amounts of sand.

## THE COLOR OF GOOD DRAINAGE

THE COLOR OF the soil in your landscape can give you some useful clues about water drainage. Dig a hole at least 2 feet deep and 2 feet wide so you can see down into it. Look at the color of the soil as you dig.

- Tinges of blue and gray indicate poor aeration, which is often the result of inadequate water drainage.

- Generally, brown soils drain much better than gray-colored soils.

- If you see browns and reds, it means your soil has oxidized iron in it. And that means that there's air and water in the pores of the soil.

## What about Weeds?

Hold on to your hoe! In your quest to rid your garden of weeds, you may be erasing some valuable information about your soil. Weeds are excellent indicators of soil conditions.

In fact, using weeds as indicators of soil quality is a well-established science—but one that's mostly used only by geologists and mining companies. But you can use it, too, and "read" your weeds to find out what's going on in the ground. You can use the information you gain in two ways:

- To plant things that will thrive in the same conditions as those weeds; or

- To amend your soil to change the conditions that made that spot so hospitable to those weeds.

Here are some general weed-reading guidelines for you to follow:

**1.** Look for large populations of the same weed, rather than just a few individual plants. One weed means nothing, but a large group of one *kind* of weed is a useful clue.

**2.** Look for more than one variety of weed before you draw any conclusions. One group of a particular "indicator weed" is only a clue. But groups of two or more weeds that like the same conditions are pretty close to absolute proof. Example: Dandelion and common mullein both indicate acid soils. However common mullein *also* indicates soil with poor fertility. So mullein alone may mean several things; but if you see both dandelions *and* common mullein in your garden, you can be *fairly* confident that your soil is acidic.

**3.** Next, consider the health of potential "indicator plants." If the weeds in question are robust, they're good indicators. Weeds that look pale or weak don't tell you much about the shape of your soil. Example: A *healthy* stand of clover may indicate soil that lacks nitrogen. The same weed will grow in soil that has adequate nitrogen, but it won't look as vigorous.

4. Weeds that keep coming back year after year are especially good indicators of soil conditions. Their environment has to be hospitable for them to survive (or reseed) from one year to the next. Once you've identified the weeds that occupy your garden in significant numbers, turn to "Tell-Tale Weeds and What You Can Grow Instead" on pages 22 and 23 to see what those weeds say about your soil. Use your newfound knowledge to change the soil conditions.

*Weeds can give you a clue as to the condition of your soil. Dandelions, for example, may mean your soil is acidic.*

## DO-IT-YOURSELF PH TESTING

HOME pH test kits are widely available and easy to use. Like most things in life, you get what you pay for—more expensive kits will yield somewhat more accurate results than the bargain-priced options. And none of them will be quite as accurate as a laboratory soil test.

But if you don't want to send your soil away to a lab and wait for the results, you can buy a home pH test kit that can give you a quick reading on your soil's pH. Most home tests involve taking a small soil sample, mixing it with distilled water, and dipping litmus paper into the resulting soil slurry. You determine your soil's pH by matching the color of the litmus paper to a color chart that comes with the kit.

# Tell-Tale Weeds and What You Can Grow Instead

Weeds, like all plants, thrive in certain types of soil. So instead of being frustrated by them, learn to recognize your weeds, dig them out, and replace them with nicer plants that like the same soil conditions.

| WEEDS | INDICATES | WHAT YOU CAN GROW INSTEAD |
|---|---|---|
| Dock, horsetail, foxtail, goldenrod, poison hemlock, sedges, Joe-Pye weed, rushes, oxeye daisy, willow | Wet, poorly drained soil | Trees and shrubs: dogwood, pussy willow, curly willow<br>Perennials: cardinal flower, yellow flag, Japanese iris, Siberian iris, ligularia, turtlehead |
| Chicory, bindweed, quackgrass, wild mustard | Compacted/crusty soil | Garden crops: bok choy, broccoli, cabbage, cauliflower, mustard |
| Dandelions, sorrel, common mullein, stinging nettle, wild mustards, wild pansy | Acid soil | Trees and shrubs: azaleas, blueberries, hydrangea, rhododendrons<br>Garden crops: endive, potatoes, rhubarb, shallots, sweet potatoes, watermelon |

Clockwise from upper left: *goldenrod, dandelions, and chicory*

| WEEDS | INDICATES | WHAT YOU CAN GROW INSTEAD |
|---|---|---|
| Field peppergrass, salad burnet, scarlet pimpernel, campion, stinkweed, nodding thistle | Alkaline soil | Trees and shrubs: lilacs |
| | | Perennials: baby's-breath, Persian candytuft, dame's rocket, dianthus, lavender, mountain pinks |
| | | Garden crops: asparagus, beets, broccoli, lettuce, muskmelons, onions, spinach |
| Daisy, wild carrot, mugwort, common mullein, wild parsnip, wild radish, biennial wormwood | Low fertility soil | Perennials: blanket flower, butterfly weed, globe thistle, pussy-toes, red valerian, sea holly, snow-in-the-mountain, thyme, yarrow |
| | | Garden crops: beans, beets, carrots, parsnips, peas, radishes |
| Chickweed, henbit, pigweed, knapweed, red clover, lamb's-quarters, purslane, wild mustards | High fertility soil | Garden crops: broccoli, corn, lettuce, melons, peppers, squash, tomatoes |

Clockwise from upper left: *salad burnet, lamb's-quarters, and mullein*

Durable, good-quality tools can take much of the toil out of soil-tending tasks.

chapter three

# Soil-Care Tools & Supplies

You may not think about having tools specifically for tending the soil. But your garden rests in a foundation of soil, and many gardening tools are made specifically for building the relationship between your plants and the soil that supports them. Whether you're digging planting holes, removing weeds, or carving a tidy edge around a flowerbed, the tools you use will make a difference in how hard you have to work.

## CHOOSE YOUR TOOLS

A sharp, sturdy, well-balanced shovel can turn the task of turning the soil into a much less burdensome chore. And a well-made cart or wheelbarrow makes all the difference when there are bags of mulch to move from the car to the garden or when there's finished compost to transport to the other end of the yard. When it comes to gardening tasks that involve digging, turning, or moving soil or soil amendments, quality tools are worth the investment.

Take your time and select tools that are made for the jobs you need to accomplish. In addition to an array of hand tools, you'll also find gas- or electric-powered versions of many tools. Whenever practical, choose hand tools rather than power tools, which are expensive, require more maintenance, and contribute to air and noise pollution. You'll enjoy your garden more if you can smell the flowers and hear the birds while you turn the soil.

If you don't already have a collection of favorite tools for working the soil, start with a few basic items and add to them as needed. By shopping for good quality and durability, you can build a small collection of tools that will serve you through a lifetime of gardening.

**Soil building goes better when you have the right tools:**

- **Wheelbarrow**
- **Spading fork**
- **Garden rake**
- **Trowel**
- **Gloves**
- **Shovel**
- **Spade**
- **Hoe**

# TOOLS TO GIVE YOUR SOIL A TURN

Unless you plan to work your soil on hands and knees, a few long-handled tools will form the core of your soil-care equipment collection. Don't scrimp on these items—these are hard-working tools, and quality really makes a difference in terms of how long they'll last and how comfortable you'll be when you're using them.

**Handle it.** Take a look at the handles of the tools you want to buy. Wood handles are strong and durable and feel good in your hands. Fiberglass handles are light and are stronger than wood. Over time, wooden handles wear slightly to become more smooth under your hands. Top-quality tools usually have handles of ash or hickory.

**The business end.** To stand up to a gardener's tough demands, a tool must be made of a very strong and durable material. That material is steel-stamped or forged. Better-quality tools feature forged steel, which is hammered into shape rather than stamped out of a sheet of metal. Hammering eliminates defects and air pockets in the metal and makes a stronger tool. Tempering is a heat treatment process that's used to strengthen both stamped and forged steel tools. Stainless steel resists rust and stays cleaner and brighter than regular (or carbon) steel, but it is also much more expensive.

**Check the connections.** Now examine the point where the handle meets the head, or blade, of the tool. No matter how sturdy the handle is, and no matter how strong the head is, if the socket that holds the two together gives way, the tool is as good as useless. The best tools have long sockets where the handle is inserted into the head and firmly fastened. This moves the stress point away from the hardest-working part of the tool and reduces the risk of the handle breaking near the

## quick tip

If you're taller than the average gardener, look for tools with *longer* handles (many sold with names like "Backsaver").

socket. Make sure the handle and head fit securely together; if there's a connection between the handle and a grip at the other end, check to see that it's sturdy, too.

## Shovel

A standard long-handled garden shovel is definitely *Shovel* a must-have soil-care tool. Its pointed edge cuts easily into hard ground (or through sod), while the rounded back of the head makes it great for digging soil out of planting holes. It's also handy for scooping up compost, gravel, sand, or other soil amendments, or for mixing cement. You can also use it to pry rocks and root clumps out of the soil. The ideal shovel should come up to your shoulder or higher. Its head should have a turned edge to protect your foot when stepping on it to push it into the soil.

## Spade

Unlike a shovel, a spade has a flat, rectangular *Spade* blade with square edges. A sharp spade makes easy work of cutting through sod and creating straight edges in soil. Use a spade for digging new beds or borders, for edging, for digging trenches, and for removing sod. A spade typically has a "D" grip at the end of its handle, which gives excellent leverage for pushing the head into sod and lifting it away. The list goes on and on for the uses of a spade, which makes it a top tool for your soil needs.

# REAL "HAND TOOLS"

NO MATTER how many tools you *buy* to tend your soil, the most important tools you'll use are a pair you already have—your hands. Although gardening tasks like transplanting and seed-sowing can be downright difficult when you're wearing gloves, many soil-care jobs lend themselves to the use of protective handwear. Whether you're spending a few hours grasping a shovel or spreading organic fertilizer around your garden, a pair of gloves makes a lot of sense when it comes to jobs that can be hard on your hands. Here are a few tips to help you shop for the strongest, most dependable hand-savers you can find:

**Material:** Are the gloves made from cowhide, goatskin, cloth, or even rubber? Many people swear by leather gloves, because they soften up after some use and don't wear out easily. Rubber is great because it's waterproof and easy to rinse clean.

**Construction:** Seams can raise blisters on your hands just as quickly as a rough tool handle. Try a glove on and move your hand around in it to feel for anything that rubs, pokes, or restricts your hand's movement.

**Care:** Can you wash and air-dry your gloves? It's important to know this before they're caked with mud. How quickly will they wear out, and can you repair them?

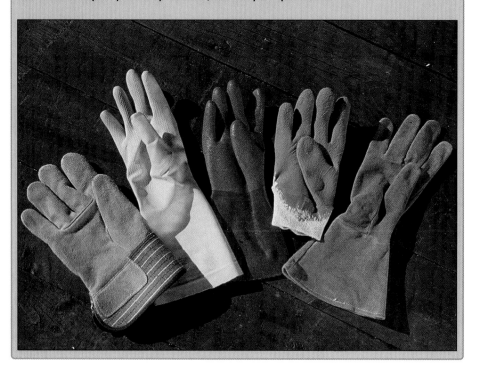

Spading fork

## Spading Fork

A spading fork's specialty is cutting into the soil with its four flat or slightly rounded tines. This type of fork is handy for mixing materials into soil and for harvesting root crops of all kinds—just make sure you don't spear a potato. An important fact to remember is that spading forks will do you little good in lifting soil, so leave that to the shovels and spades. Use a pitchfork (three long, rounded tines) or a straw fork (five to six long, rounded tines) for picking up, turning, and scattering hay mulch, leaf mold, and lightweight composted materials.

Trowel

## Trowel

A garden trowel is like a miniature shovel. It is a crucial soil tool because it makes digging holes for smaller plants and bulbs a cinch. Trowels are also great for digging up unwanted weeds in beds and borders where space is limited. When choosing a trowel, get whatever feels comfortable in your hand and will feel comfortable after an hour of use. You'll be glad to have one around when planting season comes.

## DIG THIS!

FOR AERATING established garden beds, use a broadfork (sometimes called a U-Bar digger). This tool has five straight 10-inch-long tines attached to a U-shaped bar whose two ends are the handles. You push the tines into the soil with your foot, grasp the two handles, pull them back, and the tines loosen the soil.

Garden rake

Leaf rake

## Rakes

Among the tools in your soil-care arsenal, you'll probably want to include both kinds of rake: a garden (or bow) rake and a lawn rake. What's the difference? The garden rake is a sturdy tool, with heavy-duty metal teeth that form a fierce-looking soil comb at the end of the handle. Garden rakes are perfect for leveling out ground, creating raised beds, killing emerging weeds, and spreading mulch or compost. The handle of your garden rake should be long and the business end should be heavy enough to bite into the soil easily. If you have rocky soil, choose a rake with widely spaced teeth; it will make your work less tiresome.

The lawn or leaf rake, also called a fan rake, lends itself to lighter work. Usually too flexible for moving soil or heavy mulches, lawn rakes work well when you're cleaning up or spreading lightweight mulches or smoothing the finely prepared soil on top of a seedbed. And, of course, they're perfect for collecting fall leaves to add to your compost pile or to layer atop your winter garden.

## Wheelbarrow

Who could forget the ever-useful wheelbarrow? This tool makes light work of jobs such as moving soil from one side of the yard to the other. The question to

Wheelbarrow

ask is whether you want a traditional wheelbarrow or a garden cart. A garden cart is more stable and does not tip as easily as the top-heavy wheelbarrow, but the wheelbarrow makes it easier to dump the soil where you want it. One or the other of these free-wheeling tools is essential when it's time to haul heavy loads around your landscape.

### Mattock or Pickax

Last, but definitely not least, among useful soil-tending tools is a mattock or pickax. With a pointed pick on one side of the head and a broad hoelike blade on the other, a pickax rules where the soil is rocky or full of tree roots. The head is mounted on a sturdy wooden handle that gives you great leverage for prying out rocks or loosening compacted soil. And the combination of a narrow point and a broader blade lets you pulverize small rocks and soil clods and grub out larger stones. With a mattock, you get an ax blade in place of the pick.

*Mattock*

## THE LOWDOWN ON HOES

The hoe is among the most ancient of garden tools. As such, the hoe has undergone many changes and refinements over the years. Today's hoes come in dozens of shapes and sizes, and they serve many purposes—from preparing and furrowing soil to weeding and cultivating.

**Winged Weeder.** Its innovative Delta-wing pattern is designed to cut on the push-and-pull stroke, with a gliding motion. Made of sharpened steel, the Winged Weeder comes in two blade sizes, regular and junior. Although there is only one genuine Winged Weeder brand, other manufacturers have copied the Delta-wing form with

*Winged Weeder*

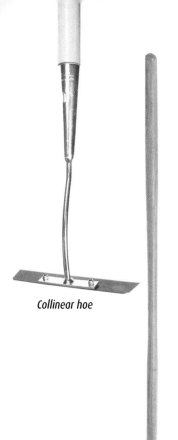

*Collinear hoe*

*Warren hoe*

greater or lesser success. Unlike the Italian hoe, this one doesn't get down and dirty; it's mainly a surface cultivator.

**Italian hoe.** This beloved hoe—with the blade held to the handle by an eye socket like an adze head—was brought to America by Italian immigrants. The Italian hoe may be fairly lightweight, with a 4 × 7-inch blade; but the blade on a truly heavy-duty model might be 8 × 8 inches, with a proportionate increase in weight. This is a great hoe for any crop: It's able to move soil quickly, and it's great for getting under the weeds.

**Collinear hoe.** The unique angle of the blade—parallel to the ground—adds to the efficiency with which this sharp steel tool skims under the surface, cutting off weeds. Like some of the other types described here, this hoe's not meant for deep-soil digging, but it's tops for taking the tops off of weeds.

**Warren hoe.** This triangular-bladed hoe, designed in the nineteenth century, is used primarily for furrowing and cutting individual weeds in close quarters. The Baby Warren, also called the onion or gooseneck hoe, has a smaller blade and is great at opening rows for onion sets. Though this hoe is good for tight spaces, generally it doesn't work well for all-day hoeing. But who wants to hoe all day anyway?

## quick tip

Save your hands from unnecessary suffering by making your own handle pads for tools. You can buy plastic-foam pipe insulation in 3-foot lengths in most hardware stores. The cushioned sleeves are slit along one side, so they slip right on to a tool handle. Simply cut 3-foot lengths of plastic-foam pipe insulation to the desired length. Then wrap it lengthwise around the handle and secure it with duct tape or electrical tape. After a few hours of tool time, your hands will thank you.

## THE TRUTH ABOUT TILLERS

Rotary tillers are unsurpassed for breaking new ground, creating raised beds, digging furrows, and mixing in soil amendments, compost, and cover crops. Whether you have a 3-acre market garden to maintain, just a few raised beds next to your patio, or something in between, you can probably use a tiller. The question you have to ask is: Which tiller is the right one for me?

### Handheld Tillers

Handheld tiller models are popular with gardeners who want an easy-to-handle, lightweight (about 20 pounds), highly maneuverable machine. A great thing about these tillers is that they are not too costly—you can find good ones for less than $300.

*Small rotary tillers are handy for preparing seed beds and for cultivating between plants.*

Handheld tillers are excellent for weeding around landscaped areas and small raised-bed gardens. You can also use them to turn compost piles. Their slim tilling width makes cultivating easy in a tight area, saving you the trouble of hand-weeding in between closely spaced garden rows.

Even though these tillers are great where space is tight and for gardeners who don't want to wrestle with a bigger machine, there are some disadvantages, too. Sod-busting takes longer with a handheld tiller, as does turning under spent crops at the season's end. And you won't go deep with these smaller tillers—most reach a maximum tilling depth of 6 to 8 inches.

### Front-Tine Tillers

Front-tine tillers can break up sod, turn under cover crops, and make quick work of weeding and cultivating tasks. Their 3- to 5-horsepower engines are easy to maintain, and because the tines are completely exposed, they're easy to remove for cleaning and maintenance—a helpful feature when you've been busting up sod.

## DON'T TILL TOO MUCH

ONE PITFALL of having a tiller is that it makes soil turning so easy that you may be tempted to do it too often. Tilling the soil and cultivating to control weeds affects everything that's in the soil, not just the intended crop. If you do decide to rev up the tiller, there are a few things you can do to minimize the damage to the soil community.

**Avoid deep tillage.** Keep organic residues (decaying plant material) in the top 2 to 3 inches of soil so microbial activity can quickly get to work to decompose them.

**Protect soil structure.** Avoid breaking up soil aggregates and ruining capillary action by pulverizing the top layers too finely or by working the soil when it's wet.

**Keep the soil loose.** Avoid compaction caused by frequent passes with heavy equipment, walking on the soil, and working soil when it's wet.

*Better balance and self-propelling drive wheels make rear-tine tillers perfect for heavy-duty tilling jobs.*

The primary disadvantage of front-tine tillers is that they are difficult to control. If you don't keep a firm grip on the handles, the machine tends to veer off in any direction it chooses, sometimes taking you with it. Along those same lines, front-tine tillers are also very hard to steer and take more muscles to turn.

### Rear-Tine Tillers

The big advantage of rear-tine tillers is that they are inherently better balanced than front-tine models. They are also self-propelled—they don't rely on the action of the tines to pull them. This makes them easy to turn; you just pivot the drive wheels and around you go.

The biggest drawback of rear-tine tillers is that they tend to be expensive; they may cost more than $600. They also take up a lot more storage room in your garage or shed than other tiller types, so there's less room for your other stuff.

## TILLER MAINTENANCE SAVES DOLLARS

ANY SIZE tiller is a major investment in garden equipment, so use these tiller-care tips to keep your tiller turning the soil at top speed:

- Keep the spark plug clean and properly gapped (check your owner's manual for details), and replace the plug annually to ensure fast starts.

- Treat the gas tank (and any storage can containing fuel) with a stabilizer each fall to prevent fuel system problems.

- Regularly lubricate the shaft with light oil for easy tine removal on handheld and front-tine models.

- Check safety controls and tine guards before each use.

- Check your drive belts (if equipped) for condition and proper tension to prevent unnecessary wear.

- Change the oil regularly for long engine life.

Three important secrets for making rich organic soil include testing your soil, adding the right amendments, and keeping your soil mulched.

chapter four

# Soil-Care Secrets

If you've been piling a lot of stuff on your garden in the hopes of super-charging your soil, you could be unwittingly changing the soil's pH level or adding too much of one nutrient and not enough of another. On the other hand, if you've been largely ignoring your soil's fertility and hoping for the best, you may be cheating yourself out of optimum harvests, a lush landscape, or the best blooms. Check out the soil-care secrets in this chapter—you won't want to ignore your soil or overfertilize it anymore!

## GETTING SERIOUS ABOUT SOIL

Let's start with one of the best-kept secrets in gardening: the inexpensive soil tests available to most North American gardeners and farmers through their local cooperative extension offices or similar agencies. In most areas, you can get a fairly comprehensive test done for between $5 and $10—less than you'd probably spend for a bag of fertilizer. And a soil test may tell you that you don't even need to add that fertilizer (or that you need to exchange it for something different)!

### Getting Tested

How you go about getting your soil tested—and the kind of information you'll get back from a soil test—depends on where you live. Start with a call to your local cooperative extension office or the soil conservation service office in your area. You'll usually find these agencies listed in the government pages of your phone book. If you find that soil testing isn't readily available in your region, ask about private testing labs near you. Three such labs are listed in "Soil Testing—The Ph.D. Level" on page 44. But get your soil tested as close to home as possible so that the recommendations you'll receive make sense for your climate and soil.

**Get your soil tested as close to home as possible so that the recommendations make sense for your climate and soil.**

37

## REQUEST A TAILOR-MADE TEST

WHEREVER you send your soil for testing, ask the lab to tailor any recommendations to a small garden (unless your "garden" covers a few acres). Lab recommendations for remedying soil deficiencies were designed to serve local farmers and thus are generally given in terms of pounds of the proposed remedy per acre of land unless you request otherwise. (If, however, you are only supplied with "pounds per acre" recommendations anyway, just divide those figures by 43 to get "pounds per 1,000 square feet.")

You should also note on the paperwork that accompanies your soil sample that you would like any remedies proposed to be in the form of organic soil amendments, as opposed to agricultural chemicals. A few weeks later, you should receive your test results in the mail.

Exactly what's included in each area's basic test will vary because: 1) each region's system is set up differently; 2) different soil scientists attach higher significance to some things and less to others; and 3) soils and their problems really do vary from one region to the next—what might be a common problem in one locale might not even be an issue somewhere else. Take salt, for example. Because salts tend to build up in western soils from their lack of rain, western labs routinely measure a soil's salt levels. In the East, however, any salts in the soil are almost always quickly washed away by rain, so eastern labs don't routinely test for them.

Such regional differences are exactly why it pays to have your soil tested by a lab in your little corner of the world (or close to it). Some state labs even (or only) send a copy of your test results to your local county extension office; that way the agents there have immediate access to your report if you call asking for guidance.

### 6 Steps to a Successful Soil Sample

When it's time to gather some soil to send off for testing, you'll want to collect a sample that represents your entire garden. Taking soil from only one spot doesn't give a very complete picture. Follow these steps to get a better sample and more useful test results:

**1.** Start with a spade, a trowel, a knife, and a bucket. Make sure your tools aren't rusty or made of galvanized (zinc-coated) metal, or they could throw off your test results.

**2.** Scrape away mulch or litter from the soil surface and use a spade to lift out a wedge-shaped piece of soil about 6 to 8 inches deep. Set the soil aside.

**3.** Now use your spade to slice a ½-inch piece of soil from the *smooth* side of your wedge-shaped hole and lift this slice out of the hole with the spade.

4. With the slice of soil resting on your spade, use the knife to cut off both sides of the slice, leaving a 1-inch-wide strip of soil in the center of the spade. Put the soil strip into the bucket.

5. Repeat Steps 2 through 4 at least half a dozen times in different parts of the garden so that the soil sample represents your *whole* garden when mixed.

6. Use your trowel to mix the soil strips together thoroughly. Fill the soil sample bag or container with some of this mixture, complete the paperwork that goes with it, and mail it all off to the lab.

To get the most accurate evaluation of your soil—and the most appropriate recommendations for different kinds of plants—you may choose to prepare separate samples from your vegetable garden soil, your lawn, and a flower garden. Of course, you'll have to pay a fee for each sample you send in for testing. Or, you can use the steps above to create a sample that includes soil from all the different sites in your landscape.

*To prepare a sample for soil testing, collect soil from several different spots in your garden. Mix the soil you gather to create a sample that represents the whole garden.*

## What Soil Tests Test For

When you get a soil test kit from your extension office and mail off your soil sample, the lab runs tests to determine what your soil's pH level is and what nutrients are found. The test results usually describe whether the nutrients are present in low, medium, high, or excessive quantities. Follow the recommendations that come with the soil test results when you need to use fertilizers or amendments to build nutrient levels in the soil, or apply the amounts listed on the package. There's no advantage to overfertilizing your soil,

# WHERE'S THE NITROGEN?

**DON'T BE SURPRISED** if your soil test results come back from the lab without a reading for nitrogen. Even though this nutrient is essential for healthy plant growth, most soil labs don't include nitrogen as part of their basic test. That's because the nitrogen content of your soil can change dramatically and quickly. If you want a test of the nitrogen in your soil, you usually have to request it; you'll pay a few dollars more for this test.

If test results show that your soil doesn't have enough nitrogen, you can help your soil and your plants by adding more organic matter in the form of compost and appropriate amounts of nitrogen-rich fertilizers such as animal manures, bloodmeal, or alfalfa meal.

and there is a good risk that you'll do more harm than good. Here are some of the nutrients most commonly tested for, along with tips on correcting deficiencies of these important plant "foods":

**Phosphorus.** Phosphorus is extremely important for healthy plant growth—without it, plants will be stunted. Sandy or shale soils that don't contain much organic matter are most likely to be phosphorus-deficient. If your soil test indicates a low amount of phosphorus, you can add bonemeal or rock phosphate to your soil and work it in to the top 6 to 8 inches. Follow the recommendations that come with your soil test results to know how much to add, and don't overdo it. Phosphorus doesn't leach out of the soil like some nutrients—once it's in the soil, it stays there. Applying too much phosphorus can throw your soil out of balance for a long time.

**Potassium.** Potassium helps plants fight disease, strengthens their stalks, and improves the quality of fruits and seeds. As with phosphorus, the soil most likely to be potassium-deficient is sandy with little organic matter. To help correct low levels of potassium,

*Organic fertilizers release their nutrients slowly, providing a steady supply of "food" for your plants without disrupting the work of beneficial soil organisms like earthworms.*

# TOO MUCH OF A GOOD THING

WHEN IT COMES to soil nutrients, experts agree that most gardeners go too far in boosting nitrogen. The result is big lush plants but few flowers or fruits. Plants will basically take up all the nitrogen you feed them, and those overfertilized plants are also more susceptible to insect and disease problems.

So, go easy on the nitrogen. An inch or so of compost per year—a little more if you have extremely sandy soil—is enough to maintain the necessary level of organic matter you need to get good yields in most northern soils.

Down South, however, it's a different story. Organic matter in the soil just burns right up in the hot, humid conditions and long growing season. As a result, southern gardeners can apply compost and manure much more freely.

And if a soil test reveals "excessive" nitrogen, simply cut back on the organic matter, grow lots of nitrogen-hungry crops such as sweet corn, potatoes, and lettuce and let the rain and those "heavy feeder" crops take care of the problem.

add manure, seaweed meal, or greensand (see "Potassium Fertilizers" on page 46) to the soil before you plant your spring garden.

**Calcium.** This mineral is a major component of a plant's cell walls. The most common soil that is low in calcium is acid, sandy soil along the sea coasts. Adding limestone to this soil type helps raise the calcium level and raises the pH, too.

**Sulfur.** Sulfur is a major part of all living organic matter, so it's no surprise that soils low in organic matter are low in sulfur. Plants need sulfur to make proteins to survive, and nitrogen needs to have enough sulfur to feed your plants. Without sulfur your plants are in big trouble, but you can easily increase soil sulfur levels by adding manures or gypsum.

**Magnesium.** Magnesium helps make up chlorophyll (the stuff that makes plants green), which helps plants make food. Sandy, acid soils may be low in magnesium and will benefit from additions of dolomitic limestone (also called magnesium lime), which also raises pH.

## quick tip

Every bag of fertilizer has three numbers connected with hyphens on the label, such as 6-2-0. Those numbers are the NPK ratio—the percentages of nitrogen, phosphorus, and potassium in the fertilizer. Organic fertilizers have lower numbers than synthetic types because the numbers show the amount of nutrients that will be available in *the first year.* Organic fertilizers release nutrients slowly, giving your plants more nutrients in the long run.

## MICRONUTRIENT TESTS: WHO NEEDS 'EM?

MICRONUTRIENTS are essential to plant health but, as their name suggests, plants use them in very small amounts. Zinc, iron, and copper are all micronutrients, and the best sources of these and other micronutrients are manure, compost, and other organic materials. If you haven't been building up your soil and your garden has visible problems, a micronutrient deficiency could be the cause. If you suspect this problem, ask that your soil be tested for micronutrients when you send in a sample. It will probably cost more than a standard soil test, but the resulting information will tell you just what your garden needs.

## THE UPS AND DOWNS OF PH

The most common factor that labs test soil for is pH level. A soil's pH is simply a measure of its acidity or alkalinity. A pH reading of 7.0 is neutral; numbers higher than 7.0 indicate your soil is alkaline; numbers lower than 7.0 mean your soil is acidic. If a soil is extremely alkaline, it doesn't matter how rich in nutrients it is because those nutrients will be tied up and your growing plants won't be able to absorb them. The ideal pH for most plants to grow in ranges from 6.2 to 7.0. This is the range where nutrients are most available for uptake by the plant's roots.

*Limestone*

If your soil is too acidic, your soil test report will probably tell you to add lime to raise the pH. But another portion of the test results should determine what kind of lime you choose. If your soil's magnesium levels are okay, the lab will probably tell you to add calcitic lime. But if your soil needs magnesium, you'll probably want to add dolomitic lime (also called magnesium lime) to correct both problems.

If your soil is too alkaline, the test results may tell you to add sulfur to lower its pH. For use as a soil

*Pelleted sulfur*

amendment you'll want to choose pelleted or granular sulfur, which is also known as garden sulfur. Stay away from the very finely ground sulfur that is sold to be mixed with water and sprayed onto plants as a fungicide. It's so finely ground that it can be a health hazard if you don't wear protective equipment when you handle it.

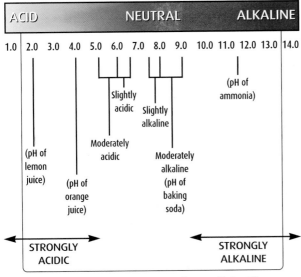

*The pH scale ranges from 1.0 to 14.0. Soils are called acidic or alkaline, but their acidity or alkalinity very rarely poses any hazard to humans. Most soils are less acidic than orange juice and less alkaline than baking soda. Gardeners generally refer to alkaline soils as "sweet" and acid soils as "sour."*

## HOW MUCH TO USE?

SUPPOSE your soil test indicates a deficiency in one or more of the major nutrients, and the report advises you to add a specific number of pounds of that nutrient for every 1,000 square feet of garden soil you need corrected. Figuring out exactly how much of a given fertilizer you need to use can seem tricky, at best.

Here's a technique you can use with any fertilizer. Let's say the lab advises you to add 2 pounds of phosphorus per 1,000 square feet of soil and you choose bonemeal as your phosphorus source. Bonemeal has a phosphorus content of about 20 percent (it should say so on the label). So you need to divide the number of pounds of bonemeal you need (2 pounds) by the percentage of nutrients in the fertilizer (20 percent). That gives you the number of pounds of fertilizer you need (10 pounds) to add per 1,000 square feet of garden space.

# SOIL TESTING—THE PH.D. LEVEL

MANY SOIL TESTING services don't provide specific organic recommendations to remedy any problems your soil test reveals, but there are a number of soil testing services that will. For a slightly higher fee than most local testing services, these labs will provide a more complete and customized package of information and instructions. They'll tell you exactly how much of which organic amendments you need to add to your soil. So if you're looking for premium, top-of-the-line organic soil testing, here are three services to consider:

**Peaceful Valley Farm Supply**

P.O. Box 2209

Grass Valley, CA 95945

(916) 272-4769

Peaceful Valley offers an initial soil test (which includes all the usual things like pH, organic matter, etc.) along with a 15-page booklet *Know Your Soil: A Handbook for Understanding Your Soil Test Report* written by noted organic farm adviser Amigo Cantisano. The booklet is keyed to your soil test results; once you have the booklet, your cost for soil tests in future years is reduced. The staff will be glad to answer your questions.

**Timberleaf Soil Testing Services**

26489 Ynez Road, Suite C-197

Temecula, CA 92591

(909) 677-7510

Timberleaf's basic soil test includes all the major plant nutrients, plus organic matter, pH, and several special tests not usually included in the lower-cost state lab packages. Your test results also include a customized report that will tell you exactly how much of any recommended soil amendments to apply, and you are entitled to one year of free consultation, as well.

**Wallace Laboratories**

365 Coral Circle

El Segundo, CA 90245

(310) 615-0116

Wallace Laboratories' "basic" soil test includes the usual things like NPK, pH ,and salinity, plus 27 other plant nutrients. Your soil is also tested for potentially toxic elements such as arsenic, aluminum, and lead.

# ORGANIC FERTILIZER OPTIONS

There are many different types of organic fertilizers to use in building healthy soil nutrient levels for healthy plants. Let's say you've just received your soil test results back and you're staring at the facts. Now what do you do? More importantly, what do you add to your soil?

## Nitrogen Fertilizers

Nitrogen promotes leafy growth, so crops like lettuce, spinach, cabbage, and lawn grass all require good doses of nitrogen. But don't overdo it on other plants, or they'll produce lots of leaves and stems and fewer flowers or fruits. Plants respond quickly to nitrogen fertilizer, so you can err on the side of caution and add more later if necessary.

*Bloodmeal*

**Bloodmeal.** The name's not pretty, but it is accurate. This fertilizer is dried and ground blood, and it's a very potent nitrogen source, so use it sparingly. If your soil's organic matter level is low, work in 3 to 5 pounds of bloodmeal per 100 square feet of soil.

**Fish meal.** A tasty soil-enriching treat of dried and ground fish scraps. Compared to bloodmeal, fish meal is usually less expensive, contains more phosphorus, and also contains many trace minerals that plants need. It also breaks down more

*Fish meal*

slowly, lasting about six to eight months in the soil. To correct soil with low amounts of organic matter, work in 3 pounds of fish meal per 100 square feet before planting.

## Phosphorus Fertilizers

Plants need phosphorus to grow strong root systems, which are vital to the overall health of the plant. Plants also need phosphorus to flower well. But phosphorus doesn't move around easily in the soil. You need to dig it in where plant roots can reach it—no deeper than the top 6 to 8 inches of the soil.

**Bonemeal.** Bonemeal is exactly what it sounds like—ground animal bones. Most bonemeals are steamed and say so on the bag, although some are raw. Steamed bonemeal supplies phosphorus faster than raw and so is more convenient for immediate phosphorus relief. Bonemeal lasts 6 to 12 months in the soil, and you should apply 3 pounds per 100 square feet if your soil is low in phosphorus.

**Rock phosphate.** Rock phosphates are the mined skeletal remains of prehistoric animals, and they release their phosphorus very slowly, over about five years. For rock phosphate to break down and be useful to plants, your soil needs to have a lot of microbial life and its pH should be 6.4 or slightly less. If your soil meets these conditions and tests low in phosphorus, apply 5 to 6 pounds of rock phosphate per 100 square feet.

## Potassium Fertilizers

Potassium helps plants function smoothly by promoting the flow of nutrients through the entire plant. It also improves the quality of fruits and seeds and helps plants withstand stress such as disease, drought, and extreme temperatures.

Bonemeal

Rock phosphate

**Greensand.** Greensand comes from a 70- to 80-million-year-old marine deposit mined in New Jersey—the only place it occurs. Greensand releases potassium very slowly over a ten-year period. It is also very rich in trace minerals, and some experts feel that these alone make greensand a worthwhile investment. If your soil is low in potassium, apply 5 pounds of greensand per 100 square feet of soil in the fall.

**Sul-Po-Mag.** It may not sound organic, but Sul-Po-Mag is the commercial name for the mined mineral otherwise known as sulfate of potash-magnesia. If your lawn needs an immediate potassium boost, this is the fertilizer for you. On low-potassium soils, broadcast about 1 pound per 100 square feet and work it into the soil.

*Greensand*

## Calcium Fertilizers

Calcium is needed in greater quantity than any other soil nutrient. And, especially in the East, it's a nutrient that's often lacking because rainwater leaches it out of the soil. A calcium deficiency can cause dieback of growing tips of plants and roots, and blossom-end rot on tomatoes and peppers.

**Limestone.** Two main kinds of limestone are used in agriculture—dolomitic and calcitic. Dolomitic limestone contains magnesium (8 percent) as well as calcium (25 percent) and should be used only if your soil test report says that you should add magnesium. Both types of limestone will boost the calcium levels in your soil gradually and will slowly raise the pH at the same time. Apply limestone with a garden spreader, adding 2 to 8 pounds per 100 square feet of soil.

*Sul-Po-Mag*

**Gypsum.** Gypsum is a mined calcium sulfate powder that will not affect your soil's pH as limestone will. Spread up to 4 pounds of granular gypsum per 100 square feet on alkaline soils that test low in calcium. In addition to helping balance your soil's nutrients, gypsum is an excellent soil conditioner: You can use it to loosen clay soil or to bind up sandy soil.

*Gypsum*

### Sulfur Fertilizers

Sulfur works together with nitrogen, and without enough sulfur, plant growth slows and leaves can turn yellow. Soils low in organic matter and with low pH levels are likely to be low in sulfur.

**Elemental sulfur.** Also known as soil sulfur or agricultural sulfur, elemental sulfur is a naturally occurring mined mineral. It works very quickly to correct sulfur deficiencies and lowers soil pH faster than any other amendment that you can apply. But be careful not to add too much to your soil. For every *full point* that you want to lower your soil pH, spread 1 pound of sulfur per 100 square feet and mix it into the top 3 inches of soil.

**Alternatives.** If you don't want to add sulfur to your soil, two other sources of sulfur are Sul-Po-Mag and gypsum. Both contain about 19 percent sulfur and would give enough to lower soil pH and release nutrients for your plants to use.

## SOIL AMENDMENTS

Adding the recommended nutrients to your soil will benefit your plants, whether they're flowers, herbs, vegetables, or grass. But that's only part of the picture. You also need to deal with the texture of your soil—whether it's heavy clay, light and airy sand, or somewhere in between.

If your soil texture test (see "Hands-On Texture Tests" on page 15) reveals problems with compaction, low humus, poor drainage, or poor water and air retention, the solution is to add organic matter. You can choose from a wide range of materials to help you boost your soil's condition, so make your selection based on the availability, cost, and ease of handling of the amendments you're considering.

**Compost.** Compost is a popular amendment because it is so cost-effective. You can buy compost or make your own. When compost is mixed into soil, the soil resists compaction and drains quickly yet still retains an enormous amount of water. Compost is very easy to spread throughout the garden.

**Leaves.** If you don't want to bother with making a compost pile and have a lot of extra leaves on the ground, you have the next best thing to compost. Just shred up those leaves and dig them into your soil. Most leaves are acidic but will not add enough acidity to significantly affect soil pH.

**Manure.** The wonder of animal manure, with its large amount of nutrients, will never cease to impress gardeners, but you should only add manure that has been aged for more than six months.

**Peat moss.** Another soil amendment that can help your garden is peat moss. Peat moss has a very low pH—3.0 to 4.5—which makes it good to spread around acid-loving plants such as rhododendrons, blueberries, and pines.

*Don't let fall leaves go to waste. Gather them in a simple wire pen for composting, or mow over them on your lawn to build the soil in your landscape.*

*Turn old news into good news by using yesterday's paper as today's mulch. Overlap the sheets to keep weeds from popping up in the cracks, and weigh the papers down with a layer of bark mulch or compost.*

## MULCH—IT'S GOOD FOR SOIL AND PLANTS

Mulching is one of the best things you can do for your gardens—whether you're growing vegetables, flowers, shrubs, or trees. Covering your soil with a thick layer of organic matter can block weed growth, keep the soil cool and moist, and—as the mulch decays—feed both the soil and the plants growing in it. But it pays to know which mulch is the right one to use in each specific gardening situation.

**Grass.** Freshly cut grass clippings are rich in nitrogen and other nutrients that will feed your plants as the clippings decompose. Warm-loving crops like peppers, tomatoes, and eggplants all do well with grass-clipping mulch. If your lawn can't supply enough grass clippings for your garden, check with a local lawn care service or a neighbor and see if you can get clippings.

**Newspaper.** Remove and recycle the slick-paper color supplements from your Sunday paper and what you've got left is a super-effective weed-suppressing mulch. Paper can keep down weeds for two summers and can be used instead of black plastic to heat up cool spring sod. Use newspaper mulch around veggies such as sweet corn, soybeans, and tomatoes. Raspberries grow well with shredded newspaper mulch, too. And the moist, dark soil under a mulch of newspaper is an earthworm paradise!

**Wood chips.** You can chip them yourself with a chipper/shredder, or buy them. The best place to use wood chips is in perennial beds and on garden paths. They're durable and work best where the soil isn't tilled or turned often. If you do use them in a vegetable garden, keep them on the surface. When turned under, wood chips can take up to a year to decompose and they tie up nitrogen so your plants can't absorb it.

**Bark.** Tree bark mulch lasts longer than wood chips because the bark sheds water rather than holding it. Bark also keeps the soil cool. Because bark has a nice appearance, use it to protect the soil in spots where you want to make a good impression—like your prized flowerbeds. Don't use bark around tomato plants; it can be harmful to them.

**Pine needles.** Pine needles can be a great mulch, and they're easy to get where pine trees grow. Boughs from spruce, fir, and pine trees make excellent

## quick tip

Don't mulch:

- in early spring when soil is still cool,

- where slugs and snails are a problem, or

- where drainage is poor.

## JUST SAY NO

COLLECTING GRASS clippings from neighbors is an easy and free way to get this high-nitrogen mulch. But there are three things you should avoid:

1. Grass or weeds that have gone to seed. Those seeds will germinate in your garden!
2. Grass from an herbicide-treated lawn. If you're not sure, either ask your neighbors whether they use herbicides, or don't use the clippings.
3. Clippings from a *freshly* cut bermudagrass or zoysia lawn—these grass clippings could take over your garden simply by rooting in moist soil! Let such clips dry out *completely* before you use them as mulch.

Straw mulch works great in the vegetable garden, where it blocks weeds and keeps the soil moist. Carrots mulched with straw will keep in the ground for winter-long harvesting.

winter mulch in northern flower gardens, protecting fall-planted pansies that you hope to overwinter and rebloom in spring.

**Straw.** Straw mulch has been proven to be a boon to tomatoes, preventing diseases such as anthracnose, leaf spot, and early blight from leaving their ugly marks on this favorite garden vegetable. Straw also works very well as an insulator, protecting crops such as carrots, parsnips, and potatoes that folks without root cellars leave in the ground during the cold months.

**Others.** Although compost, shredded leaves, and manure are most commonly used as soil amendments to add nutrients and improve soil texture, you can also use them as mulches. They provide nutrients and weed control, but many times they do more good when they're worked into the soil.

## NEWSPAPERS: FRIEND OR FOE?

ALTHOUGH NEWSPAPER is a great weed barrier, too much newspaper may not be the best news for your garden. One research study using a ½-inch layer of ground-paper pellets made from 75 percent newsprint plus small amounts of magazines and telephone books showed that the pellets caused severe reductions in the growth of marigolds, salvia, geraniums, and ageratum.

The problem appears to be the large amount of aluminum added to the paper during the manufacturing process. This aluminum can leach out of the paper mulch and prevent plant roots from absorbing phosphorus. Without this essential nutrient, plants simply can't grow well.

Some researchers recommend that home gardeners avoid using large amounts of newspaper around shallow-rooted plants in acid soils (pH less than 6.0).

# Your At-a-Glance Guide to Organic Mulches

| Mulch | Conserves Moisture | Is Durable | Prevents Weeds | On Existing Vegetable Bed | On Existing Ornamental Bed | Any Kind of New Bed | How Much to Use |
|---|---|---|---|---|---|---|---|
| Leaves | ★★★ | ★★ | ★★★ | ★★★ | ★★★★ | ★★★ | 4" loose; 1"–2" compressed |
| Grass clippings | ★★★ | ★★ | ★★★ | ★★★★ | ★★★ | ★★★★ | 4" loose; 1"–2" compressed |
| Compost | ★★★ | ★★ | ★★ | ★★★ | ★★★ | ★★★★ | 1"–2" |
| News-paper | ★ | ★ | ★★★★ | ★★ | ★★ | ★★★★ | 2 or more sheets or 6" shredded |
| Pine needles | ★★ | ★★ | ★★ | ★★ | ★★★ | ★★ | 1"–2" |
| Straw | ★★ | ★★★ | ★★★ | ★★★ | ★ | ★★ | 4" loose |
| Wood chips | ★★ | ★★★ | ★★ | ★ | ★★ | ★ | 2" small chips; 3" large chips |
| Bark | ★ | ★★★★ | ★★ | ★ | ★★★ | ★★ | 2" small; 3" large |

**KEY**
The more stars the better!

**Leaves:** Best when shredded and aged before use. Best mulch for earthworms.

**Grass clippings:** Best when dried for a day or two before use. Clippings decompose fast.

**Compost:** An inch of compost on top of the soil prevents plant diseases. Also feeds plants.

**Newspaper:** Exceptional weed preventer. Top with compost, grass, or straw to keep from blowing away.

**Pine needles:** Won't change your soil's pH when used as mulch.

**Straw:** Protects tomatoes against soil-dwelling diseases.

**Wood chips:** Ideal for pathways. Beware of treated wood chipped up and sold as mulch.

**Bark:** Most durable and attractive mulch. Don't use in your tomato patch. Beware treated wood painted to look like bark.

Clockwise from upper left: *leaves, bark, grass clippings, straw, newspaper*

With time—and turning—the layers in a compost pile blend together into a rich, soil-building concoction.

# chapter five

# Putting Compost to Work in Your Garden

It seems like magic—a pile of leaves, grass clippings, pulled weeds, and kitchen scraps turns into a dark, moist material that enriches soil and makes plants grow like crazy. But it's not magic, it's compost! And any gardener can make it with materials that are right on hand.

## WHY MAKE COMPOST?

Compost is the best material you can use to improve your soil and feed your plants. It makes the soil loose and porous and increases the amount of water your soil can hold (which helps your plants survive dry spells and droughts). Compost slowly releases nutrients into the soil, giving your plantings a steady, balanced diet to keep them growing strong. There's even evidence that adding compost to your garden protects your plants from disease.

Besides, you don't need a lot of space or time to make compost. With little effort, you can turn throwaway materials into the sweet-smelling, nutrient-rich, no-cost soil conditioner known as "gardener's gold." And when you make compost, you recycle your yard and garden wastes on site, instead of paying to have them picked up by your local hauling and recycling company. What could be better?

What happens in a compost pile is similar to what happens in your soil: Microorganisms, nematodes, and earthworms consume organic matter and break it down into simpler compounds. But in a compost pile, the process happens faster because the microorganisms have a diverse supply of raw materials to digest and absolutely prime conditions for doing their work.

> **Compost is the best material you can use to improve your soil and feed your plants.**

# HOW TO MAKE COMPOST

Raking up some fallen leaves in a corner of your yard and gradually adding garden wastes and kitchen scraps is a simple, low-tech way to compost. This laissez-faire method makes what's called *cold compost* because the pile literally stays cool. Just let the pile sit, and in about a year, you'll have sweet-smelling, dark brown, crumbly compost.

You may have seen some of your neighbors turning their compost piles and even watering them. Why do they do these things? Because they want compost fast (from start to finish in one month), so they make an *active* compost pile. The microorganisms that drive the composting process need a steady supply of water and air, and the more they get, the faster they can work.

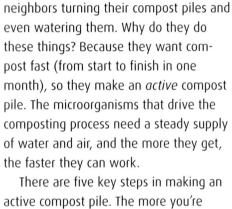

There are five key steps in making an active compost pile. The more you're willing to work with your compost, the faster it will decompose.

*Gathering materials, chopping them finely, and layering them into a pile are the first steps on the road to finished compost.*

1. **Shred and chop.** Shred or chop materials as finely as you can before mixing them into your pile. For example, you can chop fallen leaves by running your lawn mower over them. Same with kitchen scraps and the like—"the smaller the better" is always the rule for compost pile ingredients.

2. **Mix dry browns and wet greens.** The two basic types of ingredients for making compost are carbon-rich and nitrogen-rich materials. Carbon-rich materials (we'll call them "dry browns") include leaves, hay, and straw. Nitrogen-rich goodies ("wet

greens") include manure, kitchen scraps, and grass clippings (which work best in a pile when used sparsely and mixed in well so they don't mat down). Your goal is to keep a fair mix of these materials throughout your pile.

3. **Strive for size.** Build your pile at least 3 × 3 feet square and 3 to 4 feet tall so that materials will heat up and decompose quickly. Unless you have this critical mass of materials, your compost pile can't really get cooking. Check the pile a couple days after you make it—it should be *hot* in the middle, a sign that your microbial decomposers are working hard.

4. **Add water as needed.** Make sure your pile stays moist, but not *too* wet (the consistency of a wrung-out wet sponge is perfect). You may need to add water periodically.

5. **Keep things moving.** Moving your compost adds air to the mix. One way to add air is to get in there with a pitchfork and open up airholes—or, even better, move the entire pile over a few feet bit by bit, taking care to move what was on the outside to the inside of the new pile and vice versa. Or consider getting a compost tumbler—a container that moves the materials for you. A less labor-intensive way to add air is to put a homemade "chimney" in the center of the pile. (For tips on low-effort aeration, see "Aerating Compost the Easy Way" on page 69.)

*If you build a sizeable pile, keep it moist, and turn it to add air, you'll have finished compost to spread in several weeks.*

# COMPOSTING TECHNIQUES AND RECIPES

It's no secret that there are plenty of different ways to compost. As long as you're using the right ingredients—chopped or shredded "dry browns," "wet greens," air, moisture, and time—any method will work.

## Creative Collecting

Collecting materials for your compost begins, of course, at home. *Anything* organic can be composted. That includes newspapers, tea bags, and clippings from your children's haircuts as well as the usual yard and garden residue. Neighbors who collect their grass clippings may be happy to have you take them off their hands. The week after Halloween can be particularly bountiful: Cornstalks, straw bales, and leaves that stuff those easy-to-spot bright orange pumpkin-face bags that have outlived their purpose.

From there, the possibilities are truly endless. For starters, look to area businesses for materials. Orchards, factories, mills, stables, barbers, supermarkets, and restaurants all can be potential gathering grounds. Useful materials that you could find might include:

- manure or stable litter
- orchard litter
- apple pomace from cider mills
- sawdust or wood shavings
- peanut shells
- vegetable trimmings
- pet hair

## Good Old Grass and Leaves

One of the simplest techniques for making good compost requires only four ingredients: dry leaves, fresh grass clippings, water, and soil.

1. Collect dry leaves and some fresh grass clippings.

2. Mix two to four buckets of clippings with ten buckets of leaves.

3. As you work, spray the materials with a hose so that the mix feels wet, but not soggy, when you touch it. Also, add a shovelful of good garden soil as you go to introduce friendly composting bacteria to the pile.

4. Repeat Steps 2 and 3 until your pile is finished.

   If you turn this mix weekly and add more water if the pile starts to dry out, you should have rich, beautiful compost in one to two months.

## Garbage Can Compost

No space in your yard for a big compost pile? Then make compost in a can. Use a sturdy plastic or metal garbage can. Punch several holes in the bottom and sides of the can. Stand the can on bricks set in a large pan (to catch any liquid that might drain out). Layer 3 inches of soil, 2 to 3 inches of kitchen scraps, and then 2 inches of grass clippings, shredded newspaper,

*Sturdy, moisture-resistant cinder blocks make a strong bin, and you can turn them to let in air through their holes or use them as planters around the top of the bin.*

## COMPOST INGREDIENTS

### High-Carbon "Dry Browns"

Dry leaves

Dry weeds

Straw

Hay

Chopped cornstalks

Aged sawdust

Nutshells

Paper (moderate amounts)

### High-Nitrogen "Wet Greens"

Vegetable scraps

Fruit scraps

Coffee grounds

Tea bags

Fresh grass clippings

Fresh leaves (avoid walnut and eucalyptus)

Freshly pulled weeds

Hair (pet and human)

Manure (cow, poultry, horse, pig, rabbit)

Seaweed

WHILE YOU'RE BUILDING super soil with compost, there's a good chance that you're also helping to protect your garden from many common plant diseases. There's plenty of scientific evidence that compost helps prevent disease.

- In Pennsylvania, applying compost to alfalfa fields that had suffered from disease problems resulted in a doubling of yields.

- A New York country club used compost to combat turf diseases and cut fungicide use by 97 percent in just three years!

- In Florida, compost is being use to protect peppers, squash, peas, and green beans from diseases.

- In Ohio, composts that help to eliminate soil-borne diseases in potted nursery plants are being produced on a large commercial scale.

To get the maximum disease-preventive benefit from compost, use compost as a mulch rather than digging it in.

or chopped leaves. Repeat the layers until the can is full, finishing with a layer of soil. The finished compost will be ready in about three to four months—with no turning required! One caution: With this method, the compost may produce odors as it breaks down, so put the can in an out-of-the-way spot.

### Terrific Tumbler Compost

The secret to success with a compost tumbler (shown below) is to stockpile materials until you have enough to fill the tumbler. Here's the technique:

**1.** Start stockpiling kitchen wastes in a 20-gallon garbage can (put the can right by your tumbler). In about two weeks, you should have enough for a batch of compost.

**2.** Transfer the kitchen wastes to the tumbler drum, and add equal volumes of chopped leaves and fresh grass clippings.

**3.** Rotate the tumbler a few times each day for two weeks. (You should also be stockpiling a new batch of kitchen wastes during this time.)

*Compost tumblers make turning a breeze. Just fill them with a balanced mix of moist and dry materials and start spinning.*

**4.** Unload finished compost and load in new materials to start the next cycle.

When you reach October, you can load the tumbler one final time. That batch will be ready at about the end of the following April, and you can begin the two-week routine again.

### Cold Weather Composting

When the weather turns cold in the fall, you can still keep your compost pile working by insulating it. Simply gather bags of fallen leaves from the curbsides around your town and heap them in a circle about 4 feet in diameter around a low compost pile. The bags provide some heat, the contents of the bags will decompose slightly, and the center of the circle should stay unfrozen all winter, so you can keep dumping your kitchen scraps there.

You can also insulate a compost bin by piling straw bales around it and covering the whole thing with a large sheet of plastic.

## USING COMPOST TO ENRICH YOUR SOIL

Sometimes, people get the idea that they need to bury their gardens under truckloads of compost, but that's not true. A surprisingly moderate layer of compost will produce wonderful results. Here are some basic guidelines for how much compost to apply to enrich your soil.

- In most areas of the country, a yearly rate of just ½ inch of compost containing 1 percent nitrogen (about four 40-pound bags or 30 gallons per 100 square feet) will provide ample nutrients for excellent plant growth.

- In the longer growing seasons of the South and in areas with very high rainfall, double the rate to 1 inch per year.

> ## quick tip
>
> Save vegetable peelings, eggshells, coffee grounds, tea bags, and apple cores for the compost pile (just keep a plastic bucket with a lid on the kitchen counter for collecting them).
>
> If you have big, fat kitchen leftovers such as broccoli stalks, corn cobs, and uncooked pumpkin rinds, slice or chop them up before you add them to your compost (unless you want to see a really scary jack-o-lantern smiling up at you in the spring). Citrus peels need to be cut into especially small pieces—1-inch strips—or they won't break down.

## quick tip

Once you've been composting for a year, you can celebrate your success by sharing your experiences with readers of *Organic Gardening* magazine in the 'Compost Corner' section. Write the magazine at Compost Bin, *OG*, 33 E. Minor Street, Emmaus, PA 18098 with a description and a photo of your compost pile. You'll receive their nifty compost pin award in return.

- For one-time applications to new garden beds, mix 1 to 2 inches of mature, finished compost 4 to 5 inches deep into the soil. For new garden beds in the Deep South or high rainfall areas, double that initial "new bed" application to 2 to 4 inches.

- If you live in a very cold, short-season area (Zone 4 or colder), where the nutrients in compost aren't used up or leached away as fast, start with 1 inch for new beds, then add slightly less than ½ inch annually.

### Checking Compost Quality

Compost is the ideal soil conditioner because it has such a high organic-matter content: 30 to 60 percent. But if you buy commercial bagged or bulk compost, be wary. Tests done for *Organic Gardening* magazine found that many bagged composts contained less than 30 percent organic matter (OM). Here's a nifty way you can estimate the OM content of a sample of compost.

Spread out a shovelful of compost indoors on a thin layer of newspaper and let it air-dry for about a week. Then, measure exactly 2 cups of the dried compost and weigh it. If it weighs between 8 and 12 ounces, then it contains the desired level of organic matter. If

*Topping your garden beds with a layer of finished compost is a great gift to your soil and plants. Even a layer only 1 inch thick will add valuable nutrients and organic matter.*

it's less than 8 ounces, the compost is immature; if it's more than 12 ounces, it's too old or diluted with soil.

If you live in a dry climate or have alkaline soil (a pH above 7), you also need to be careful about the salt levels of any compost you plan to use in large quantities. Homemade composts, especially those made from a good mixture of ingredients, rarely develop high salt levels—*unless* you happen to be using large amounts of manure (cattle are often fed lots of salt to make them gain water weight).

## How to Add Compost

To improve fertility and soil structure in new garden beds, mix the compost in as deep as you can. If you're double-digging your soil (see "Double-Digging Delivers Double-Good Beds" on page 72 for directions) or plan to plant crops close together for an intensive garden, you'll also want to mix your annual booster doses of compost into the soil because this technique encourages plant roots to grow deeper than usual.

When your aim is to use compost to fight plant diseases, leave your compost on the surface of the soil, especially if you garden in the South, where diseases tend to be more frequent and severe. It's also a good technique for small vegetable gardens, where it's not easy to rotate your crops from year to year. It's also a good idea to keep disease-prone plants such as tomatoes and roses mulched with compost at all times.

## When to Apply Compost

If you plan to mix compost into your garden soil, the best time is about two to four weeks before you

# COMMUNITY COMPOST

MANY CITIES and towns have a composting center where they produce compost on a huge scale, and they usually give it away free to local homeowners! Check to see whether your municipality has a composting center. If not, you can also check with large garden centers in your area—they'll usually deliver bulk compost to your home for a fee.

Before you load up on local compost or order it from a garden center, inspect it. Compost should be dark and crumbly and not contain visible wood chips. The smell should be nicely "earthy," with no hint of ammonia or sourness.

Shape a rounded pen from a roll of wire fencing and some chain snaps, and you'll have an instant compost container that you can move to any place in your yard. You'll need at least 10 feet of 36- to 48-inch-wide fencing, and three or four snaps or clips to hold the ends together. Toss in yard waste, kitchen scraps, and garden refuse, and you're on your way!

begin planting. If you're planning to spread compost on the surface of your garden soil as a disease-preventing *mulch,* you have two choices. You can either do so several weeks *before* you plan to plant, or wait until *after* your seeds have sprouted and the young plants are up and growing. That's because fresh compost can inhibit the germination of some seeds—especially beans, carrots, and onions.

## BINS, FRAMES, AND TUMBLERS

Although a bin or frame isn't essential for making good compost, it does have advantages. Here are some reasons why you might want to invest in making or buying a container for your compost.

**Out of sight, out of mind.** If you have a small yard and have to make compost in full view of your neighbors, you (and your neighbors) may be happier if your compost is under cover. (If you face this situation, see "Camouflaging Your Compost" on page 66.)

**Bins help boost production.** Compost bins help you organize your composting system. For example, with a three-bin system, you can pile slowly decomposing yard wastes in one bin, mix kitchen scraps and finely chopped materials for a fast compost pile in another bin, and keep your finished compost in the third. Or use one bin for finished compost, and turn your compost-in-progress from one of the remaining bins to the other.

**Tumblers make for easy turning.** Special compost tumblers are a great choice if you don't want to struggle with turning compost by hand.

### Build-It-Yourself Bins

You can build a compost bin of almost any durable material, including cinder blocks, straw bales, chicken wire, snow fencing, or wood.

**Pallet bin.** Recycled hardwood pallets provide a quick, easy—and often free—compost bin. Just stand

the pallets on end in a square, pound in
fence posts to hold the corners together, and use heavy gauge wire to
fasten the pallets to the posts.

**Cinder-block bin.** When building a
bin with cinder blocks, stack the blocks
three or four high to form a U-shaped
bin, leaving 1-inch spaces between the
blocks to allow good airflow.

## Ready-Made Bins

Buying a ready-made compost bin
may cost you more than buying materials for a do-it-yourself bin. However,
ready-made bins are quite attractive
and durable, and they certainly save
you time and effort compared to
making your own.

**Pen-type composters.** Many of
these composters are made of recycled
plastic, which won't warp or discolor
like wood. Bins made of dark-colored
plastic catch and hold the sun's heat,
making them good choices for those
who live in frigid climates. You can also
buy an inexpensive—and compostable—
cardboard container that will hold your
compost for about a year before it's
ready to become one with its contents.
At that point, you can just toss it into
another cardboard bin and start again!

**Compost tumblers.** Tumbler or drum
composters are plastic or metal containers that are
usually mounted on elevated frames, and they're easy
to rotate. Some models have gear-driven turning
mechanisms; others spin on ball bearings. Another
type resembles a boulder-size metal or plastic ball. To

*Compost happens, whether you
make it in a wire pen (top),
a cinder-block bin (middle), or
a purchased bin made of recycled plastic (bottom).*

*This tumbler turns your compost as you roll it around your yard, giving you and your compost an aerobic workout.*

turn the contents, you just roll the sphere around on the ground.

One drawback of using a compost tumbler is that, once the tumbler is filled to the proper extent, you have to stop adding fresh ingredients to allow the composting process to complete. The process usually takes about two weeks, and during that time, you need to stockpile materials in another container or area.

## CAMOUFLAGING YOUR COMPOST

Although your compost pile is a vital part of your garden, it's not usually a sight that you want in full view. Don't worry; there are lots of creative ways to dress up a compost pile. Here are just a few to get your imagination working:

- Plant a border of fast-growing annuals such as sunflowers, tall cosmos, or nicotiana in front of your compost to conceal a work-in-progress.

- Let your climbing vegetables use your wire compost bin for support. Early peas, followed by beans and then a fall pea crop will cover the bin—productively—for the entire season. Scarlet runner beans, planted every third plant, add a bright red-orange glow to the whole display.

- If you're not a vegetable fan, plant morning glories around a wire bin. The vines will climb the support just as well, and greet you with beautiful flowers every morning.

- Make compost bins out of pallets laid sideways, so a closed end faces up and the open ends are on the sides. Then top the pallets with flower boxes or wallpaper-soaking trays planted with trailing vines.

- Position your compost pile at the center of your garden, and build tall raised beds on three sides. Not only will they provide camouflage, they'll also offer some insulation, so your active composting season will last longer.

- If you have some extra compost that you're not ready to use yet, try planting a camouflaging crop right on top of it. You can grow a green manure crop to produce even more soil-enriching material (see "Full-year green manure" on page 92 to learn about green manure crops), or try planting melons or pumpkins.

*If you live in the woods, you may be able to collect enough logs to make a sturdy, rustic-looking frame that camouflages the compost inside it.*

## JUMP-STARTING YOUR COMPOST PILE

Sometimes a compost pile just seems to get stuck, and things won't break down. Here are some tactics to try if your compost just won't cook:

**Make a bigger pile.** Check the dimensions of your compost pile. To make hot compost, your pile should be at least 3 × 3 feet square and 3 to 4 feet high. If your pile is smaller than that, you'll probably have to be content with making cold compost.

*"Turning" compost—lifting and mixing the ingredients with a spading fork—is a time-honored and effective way to promote decomposition.*

## quick tip

If raccoons, opossums, or some other scavenging animal has been tearing at your pile, you'll find it's hard to break them of the habit. (Remember not to add meat scraps or fat to your pile!) Your best bet is to make a sturdy cover for your pile, or to buy a completely enclosed bin or tumbler to keep garbage hounds away.

**Soften things up.** If the residues in your pile are too tough, they won't break down. Take a look at the contents of your pile. If you find lots of woody material, or coarse, dry leftovers such as corncobs, mix in some succulent plant material (like freshly mowed grass clippings) or some fresh manure. Try to build your pile in layers, alternating "brown" (carbon-rich materials like dry leaves and straw) and "green" (nitrogen-rich materials like fresh grass clippings and food scraps). If you don't have the time to turn your pile, layering your pile and adding some rich topsoil, finished compost, or manure to the pile will ensure that you will have compost—it will take longer than if you turned the pile but you'll still have the desired end product!

**Water it down.** When your pile is too dry, it will have a whitish, powdery deposit inside. If you spot this when you're turning your compost, add water until a sample handful feels moist, but not wet enough to squeeze excess water from.

**Add a dry touch.** If your pile is too wet, add dry soil and/or turn the pile to dry off excess water. A pile may also stay wet if it gets compacted. If your pile always seems to be too wet, try adding a layer of coarse material such as straw right in the center of the pile.

**Cover it up.** If all else fails, or if the weather turns cold, insulate your pile by covering the top of it with hay or black polyethylene plastic.

## What to Do about Stinky Compost

On rare occasions a compost pile seems to go rotten, and it will develop a nasty odor. If your compost smells bad, don't apply it to your soil. Instead, fix the conditions that created the smell—it's easy to do. If your pile smells sour or like rotten eggs, it's probably too wet and doesn't have enough air circulating in it. Spread the compost out, fluff it up, add some more dry ingredients, and let it sit for a few weeks. Once it smells better, it's fine to use.

If you notice an ammonia smell, there's too much nitrogen in the material. Mix in some dry brown material such as straw, sawdust, or leaves, and let the pile age until it develops that good earthy aroma.

## Aerating Compost the Easy Way

One way to get air into your compost pile without a lot of shoveling is to provide a central "chimney," or a column of air that gets down into the center of the pile. You can make a chimney by drilling holes into a PVC or metal pipe. Then poke the pipe right into the center of your compost pile.

Another way to create air spaces inside a compost heap is to lay 1- to 2-inch-diameter perforated pipes across the pile as you build it. When the pile is finished cooking, just pull out the pipes.

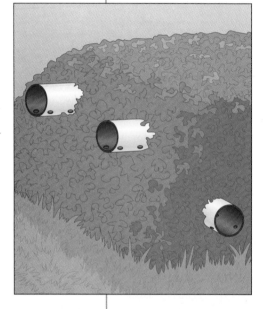

*Another way to get air into your pile without turning the compost is to lay perforated pipes across the pile as you build it.*

## WHAT'S MUSHROOM COMPOST?

MUSHROOM COMPOST is the stuff that mushroom farmers grow mushrooms in. It's a blend of one-third horse manure, one-third spoiled hay, and one-third ground corncobs. It contains nitrogen, potassium, and phosphorus (three essential nutrients for plants), and the pH is near neutral, so it's an excellent soil amendment.

Organic mushroom compost, by the way, is what you want. It's steam-treated to kill weed seeds and competing fungi and molds; some other mushroom composts are chemically treated.

Digging may not be your favorite pastime, but if you take the time to work and prepare the soil at the start, you'll end up doing less digging and other maintenance in the long run.

# chapter six

# From Ground to Garden

If gardening were a board game, we'd all skip "start" (digging a new bed) and go straight to "win" (enjoying the results). But the old gardening wisdom is true: If you prepare the soil well in the beginning, you'll save time later on weeding, feeding, watering, and other chores. And your plants will reward you with robust health that promotes natural insect and disease resistance.

## DIGGING IN

There are as many ways to start a garden as there are gardeners. And there are also ways to make this task considerably easier. How you go about preparing your garden bed depends on a number of things, including the condition of the soil when you start and what you want to grow.

For example, double-digging is one of the best ways to build a raised vegetable bed. But if you plan to plant perennials, you can use a less work-intensive method of bed preparation, or even a no-dig method. Whatever bed preparation method you choose, remember that your goal for any kind of garden is healthy, balanced soil that holds the right amounts of air, water, and nutrients.

Before you dig in, read on, and use your answers to the following questions to help you decide which garden-making method will work best for you:

- What do you plan to grow in your garden?
- What type of soil and soil problems do you have to begin with?
- How hard are you willing, or able, to work?
- How soon after preparing the garden do you want to plant?

> **Your goal for any kind of garden is healthy, balanced soil that holds the right amounts of air, water, and nutrients.**

Step 1

# DOUBLE-DIGGING DELIVERS DOUBLE-GOOD BEDS

There's no question that it's hard work, but double-digging is still one of the absolute *best* ways to prepare a garden bed. You loosen the soil to about 24 inches deep when you double-dig, which gives your plants' roots lots of room to roam. Double-diggers who've examined the benefits of this method report that they get much higher yields from double-dug beds—in some cases, 9 to 15 *times* the yields of similar-size-but-not-double-dug plots!

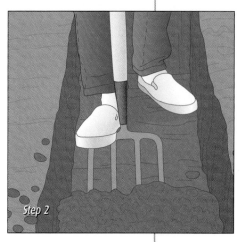
Step 2

1. Using a spade or sharp shovel, dig a trench about 1 foot wide and 1 foot deep across the narrow end of the bed. Put *this* soil (and *only* this trench's worth of soil) into a wheelbarrow. This soil will be used to fill in the last trench when you're all done digging.

2. Loosen the soil in the bottom of that trench an additional 12 inches with a spading fork. Push the tines of the fork in to their full length, then use the handle as a lever and push down to move the tines up through the soil.

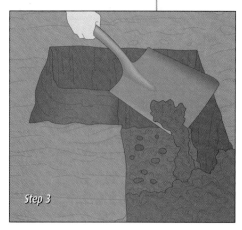
Step 3

3. Now dig a second trench, also about 1 foot deep and 1 foot wide, next to the first trench. Use this second trench's soil to fill the first trench.

# DIGGING DOS AND DON'TS

## Dos

- Warm up with a brisk ten-minute walk and a good stretch before you begin. Digging is a strenuous activity.

- Keep your knees slightly bent when you dig to avoid injuring your back. Hold the filled shovel close to your body as you work. Let gravity work in your favor by keeping the shovel's blade—not the handle—vertical as you push it into the soil.

- Take frequent breaks to rest your back. Stand with your hands on your hips and lean back gently for a few seconds.

- Wear sturdy shoes or boots to protect your arches from bruising during repeated foot-powered shovel assaults on rocky or sod-covered soil. A pair of sturdy, comfortable gloves are nice to have, too.

- Use sharp, sturdy tools. And choose the right tool for the job. (See "Soil-Care Tools & Supplies" on page 25 for tips on tools to use for tending the soil.)

- Size your garden bed so that you can plant and weed it without walking on the soil. A 3-foot-wide bed will allow you to reach easily into the middle from either side.

- Plan your gardens wth permanent paths. If you're making raised beds, dig the good soil out of the pathways and add it to the planting areas. Mulch the paths heavily and walk on them between your gardens.

- Add amendments last by spreading them over the surface and forking or raking them into the top 3 to 4 inches of soil. A rule of thumb is to add 1 inch of organic matter, such as compost or well-rotted manure, to a garden bed every year.

- Keep your feet out of your garden beds to avoid compacting the soil you've worked so hard to improve.

- Use stepping stones, a broad plank, or even a piece of cardboard for those times when you just *have* to step onto your newly dug soil. By distrbuting your weight more evenly, you'll avoid undoing your digging.

## Don'ts

- Try to do too much at one time. If you plan to double-dig your vegetable garden, add just one or two double-dug beds to your garden each year until you've prepared the entire area.

- Dig your garden when the soil is wet. Working wet soil does serious damage to its structure.

- Step on your newly dug beds and compact your loose, fluffy soil.

- Till or dig your beds every season. Earth-worms and other beneficial soil microor-ganisms are happier—and more helpful—if they aren't disturbed.

Step 6

4. When the second trench is empty, use the fork to loosen the lower 12 inches of soil in it, just as you did in the first trench.

5. Repeat these steps, trench by trench, until you reach the other end of the garden bed.

6. After you've removed the top layer and loosened the lower layer of soil in the last trench, use the soil you saved in the wheelbarrow from the first trench to fill in this trench. Rake the whole

## DON'T TILL TOO MUCH

ROTARY TILLERS are great for saving time and your back. They can make short work of sod-busting and are tops for turning under cover crops. But overusing them in the garden is harmful to your soil.

Too many tiller turns around the garden pulverizes the soil and destroys its structure. Tilling also reduces the organic matter content of your soil by speeding up decomposition of the soil's organic reserves. Tilling is also hard on earthworms—the whirling tines chop up some worms and leave others exposed to drying sun and wind. And if you have perennial weeds like quackgrass or Canada

thistle that have spreading root systems, dig them out of your beds before you till. If you don't remove these wily weeds first, the tiller will chop the root systems into small pieces and create a bed full of newly sprouted weeds.

Use your tiller for big soil-turning tasks, but look to other tools when you can. For example, a garden rake is better for mixing in soil amendments, and a sharp hoe is the tool of choice for routine cultivation.

bed level from outside the bed, so you won't step on the freshly "double-dug" soil.

Step 7

7. Spread a 1-inch layer of compost over the entire bed for a nutrient boost and to prevent diseases.

8. Place your plants in your newly double-dug bed! Don't step on the bed or you'll compact the loose fluffy soil. If you can't reach the center of the bed, get a sturdy board and lay it on supports resting outside the garden so it extends over the top of the bed. Stand or kneel on the board when you're ready to plant in the middle of your garden.

## ANOTHER WAY TO MAKE YOUR BED

Some people look at their lawn and see, well, grass. Others see spaces where new flowerbeds and mixed plantings could be. If your interest in the soil involves ways to use it to support more flowers, read on to learn the steps to follow to turn boring expanses of sod into pretty perennial gardens.

1. We've said it before, but it's worth repeating: *Don't dig in wet soil*. Start your bed-building venture by checking to make sure the soil is dry enough to dig.

2. To create a straight-edged bed, drive stakes into the ground and stretch a clothesline from stake to stake to mark off the perimeter of the garden. You can outline a bed with a curved edge by laying a garden hose on the ground and adjusting it to the desired shape. To mark the edges before you remove the sod, drive your garden fork into the ground along the outline of the rope or hose, and break up the sod as you go.

**How can you tell if your soil is too wet to work? To check, scoop up a fistful of soil and squeeze it. If the ball of soil crumbles and falls apart, the soil is dry enough for digging. If it sticks in a lump in your hand, wait a few dry days and try again.**

**3.** If you don't plan to use the sod in another spot in your landscape, a garden fork is a good tool for turning the sod and the soil. You can also use a sharp shovel or spade for this task, but you may find the work easier with a fork because it's easier to push the tines into the soil.

**4.** To lift the sod, push the fork straight down into the ground with your foot, then use the handle as a lever to pry loose a clump of sod. Grab the sod and shake the soil from the roots onto the bed. Throw the remaining grass on your compost pile and repeat until you've uncovered the soil over the entire bed. (If this is harder work than you can do and you're willing to wait a few months to plant, see "Building a Lazy Bed" on page 78.)

*Before you dig a new bed, scoop up some soil and squeeze it. If the soil crumbles, it's dry enough for digging (top).*
*A garden fork is a good tool to use to turn the sod and soil because it's easy to push the tines into the ground (bottom).*

**5.** If you haven't already tested the soil in this new garden bed, now is the time to take a sample to send off for analysis. It's definitely worth it to do this now, before you invest time and money in fertilizers and amendments for your new bed. See "6 Steps to a Successful Soil Sample" on page 38 for tips on taking a soil sample.

**6.** Before planting, spread approximately 1 inch of compost or composted manure over the top of the bed. This is also the time to blend in any of the amendments that were recommended as a result of the soil test. Then use your fork to mix them 12 to 18 inches deep into the loosened soil.

**7.** When the soil is light and fluffy and the amendments are mixed in, grab a garden rake and level the surface of the soil with the tines. Then flip the rake over and smooth the soil with the backside of the rake. Now you're ready to plant.

**8.** Perennials of all shapes and sizes come in plastic nursery pots. The trick to un-potting them without damaging the roots is to turn the pot upside down, then cradle the soil surface and plant in one hand while gently squeezing the pot with the other until the roots and soil slide out. Untangle any roots that are circling the rootball. Then use a trowel to dig a hole deep enough to set the rootball of the plant at the same depth it sat in the pot. Make the hole wide enough so there's room to straighten out any long roots. When the plant is in its hole, firm the garden soil around the rootball. Then create a shallow trench around the root zone on the surface of the soil so water will collect and trickle down to the roots. Fill a watering can with water and soak the soil around each plant's roots.

*Now is the time to get your soil tested before you spend money on fertilizers (top left). Once you get the results, blend in any of the recommended amendments before planting (top right).*

*You can cover a top layer of compost with an attractive organic mulch (above).*

**9.** When your plants are set in place and watered well, cover the ground around and between them with a 2-inch layer of compost. If you like, you can top the compost layer with an inch or two of a more attractive organic mulch, such as pine needles, buckwheat hulls, or shredded bark.

*The last step in preparing a bed is edging, which helps keep grass roots from invading the bed.*

**10.** Edging your bed gives it a neat, finished look and has the practical advantage of keeping grass roots from taking hold in the bed's soft, fertile soil. Here's an easy and effective way to edge: Take a half-moon edger and push it straight down into the soil all along the edge of your bed. (These edging tools are inexpensive and really easy to use—the 4-inch length digs to exactly the depth of grass roots, and the curved blade is easy to push in.) Rock the edger back and forth to cut the sod.

When you've made a straight cut around the whole perimeter of the bed, make a second cut on the flowerbed side, but this time push the edger in toward the first cut at a 45-degree angle. Pull out the wedge of sod and soil, leaving a narrow, V-shaped trench around the bed. This keeps grass roots out of your beds because when the roots break through the straight side of the trench and contact air, they will turn around and grow back into the soil on the lawn side of the trench. Over time the roots will weave through and reinforce the wall of the trench, without invading your garden.

## BUILDING A LAZY BED

If you plan to put in a new bed several months before you plant it, why not take it easy and take advantage of the time you have to create a "lazy bed"? This no-digging method is easier on your back and kinder to the soil because it preserves the existing structure, pores, and worm tunnels. And with this method you'll end up with a raised bed, which will drain well and warm up quickly in the spring.

Start by mowing the sod or weeds or whatever is growing in your intended site as low as your mower will cut. This is the one time when it's okay to "scalp" the grass with your mower. Then completely cover the close-cropped sod with several thicknesses of newspaper. It helps to wet the newspaper to keep it from blowing away as you're laying it out.

Top the newspaper layers with 8 to 10 inches of organic matter. Be creative and thrifty and use materials that you have on hand or that are easy to come by. Shredded leaves, compost, grass clippings, wood chips, straw or hay, and even kitchen scraps are all fair game here. Just pile it on and wait for these riches to break down into healthy soil for future planting. Keep in mind that if your lazy bed is in a spot that you look at often, you'll want to top it with something that looks nice while you're waiting— choose a "pretty" mulch like wood chips or cocoa shells for the top layer. If looks are less of a concern and rich soil is the ultimate interest, tuck all that organic matter under a layer of black plastic for quicker decomposition.

If you build your lazy bed in late summer and let it "cook" until spring, it should be ready for planting when the local nurseries put their plants out for sale. While you wait, use your time to browse through glossy plant catalogs and make a map of exactly what you want to plant in the soft, rich soil of your new bed.

## RAISE YOUR GARDEN IN RAISED BEDS

Few methods of gardening offer as many advantages as growing in raised beds. Raised garden beds are higher than ground level and are separated by paths. Plants cover the bed areas, and gardeners work from the paths. Typical raised beds are 3 to 5 feet across to permit easy access from the sides and may be

### quick tip

One way to dress up a lazy bed while you're waiting for it to decompose into the garden of your dreams is to tuck potted plants into the mulch. Pots of flowering bulbs, bright-colored annuals, or even potted perennials will look like they're growing in your new garden—just hide their pots in the thick layer of organic matter. An added benefit is that the containers will need less watering because the mulch will help them hold moisture.

*Improved drainage, space savings, and increased productivity are just a few of the advantages of raised-bed gardening.*

any length. You can grow vegetables in raised beds, as well as herbs, annual or perennial flowers, berry bushes, or even small trees. Raised beds can solve problems of difficult soils; improve production; save space, time, and money; and improve your garden's appearance and accessibility.

Raised-bed crops are more productive because they grow in deep, loose, fertile soil that is never walked upon. And you can grow twice as many crops in the same space: In a row garden, the crops occupy only one-third of the garden area while the paths between the rows take up two-thirds of the space. In a raised bed garden, the proportions are reversed.

First clear the site and remove weeds or sod, then use one of the following techniques to build your beds:

**Mounding.** This is the quickest and easiest way to make a raised bed. Simply till or fork up the soil to loosen it, then heap compost, well-rotted manure, and other organic matter on top and rake it together to create a mounded bed. If your soil is very poor or rocky, use purchased topsoil mixed with compost and amendments to build the beds from the ground up.

Because a freshly built mounded bed is loose and full of air, it settles initially and can easily erode. Add more soil-compost mix if the bed loses height. Frame the bed if erosion is a problem.

**Tilling and hilling.** This bed-building method prepares the soil almost as thoroughly as double-digging but takes much less time.

## quick tip

Don't build frames for your garden beds or compost bins from pressure-treated CCA wood—chromium, copper, and arsenic are toxic preservatives that leach into the soil from such wood. Instead, choose rot-resistant woods such as cedar, black locust, or oak, and line the inside of the wooden frame—where it comes in contact with the soil—with heavy-duty black plastic.

1. With a rotary tiller, thoroughly till the entire garden area to a depth of 6 to 8 inches.

2. Using stakes, twine, and a tape measure, lay out the perimeter of the beds. Be sure you leave adequate space for pathways. From this point on, walk only in those pathways, not on the marked beds.

3. Loosen the subsoil in the marked-off areas with a garden fork.

4. Next, using a spade, scoop up the top 2 to 3 inches of soil from the pathways around the beds, and add it to the beds to produce nicely raised beds.

*For extra planting space, fill the holes in a cinder-block raised-bed frame with soil, or drive stakes in them to support vining crops in your garden.*

## MAKE AN INSTANT-GRATIFICATION GARDEN

DON'T WANT TO WAIT while a thick layer of organic matter breaks down before you plant stuff in your new bed? Modify the lazy bed technique to get a garden you can plant right away, without intense digging! Cover your intended bed with a thick layer of wet newspaper, just as you would for a lazy bed. Then cover the whole plot with a 4- to 6-inch-thick layer of equal parts soil and compost mixed together. (Many garden centers sell this "topsoil" and will deliver a truckload to you.)

Now you can sow seeds or set transplants of shallow-rooted annual flowers and vegetables right into the top layer of your lazy bed. In a couple of months, the newspapers will have completely smothered the grass and will be decomposed enough for deep-rooted plants to penetrate the paper and root in the soil beneath the sod. And earthworms will gradually mix the rich topsoil deeper into the bed.

*Handsome crimson clover is one of several soil builders you can sow to help prevent nutrient deficiencies and to add organic matter.*

# chapter seven

# Advanced Soil Management

Care for the soil, and the soil will care for your plants. Plants growing in healthy, organically managed soil are lush, green, and vigorous. In contrast, plants growing in poor soil that lacks nutrients are often small and weak, sometimes even discolored, stunted, and deformed. Not a pretty sight!

## SIGNS OF SOIL TROUBLE

In this chapter you'll learn to recognize some of the signals from plants that indicate nutrient deficiencies in the soil. And you'll discover how to use special plants called cover crops to build the richest soil ever. These techniques rely upon the same principle we told you about in "Healthy Soil, Healthy Plants" on page 1: Healthy soil yields healthy plants.

Just as your doctor studies your symptoms to figure out the cause of an illness, gardeners learn to diagnose plant problems by looking for key signs. When nutrients are lacking in the soil, your plants will tell you. Not with words, of course, but by displaying symptoms that often point directly to the missing nutrient.

Some of these nutritional deficiencies look very similar, so to confirm your diagnosis, you may want to have your soil tested (that way you'll save the time and cost of adding nutrients that your soil doesn't need). And remember that overdoing nutrients can cause just as many problems as deficiencies can—more is definitely not better where fertilizers are concerned. Here are six deficiencies and what to do about them.

> **Overdoing nutrients can cause just as many problems as deficiencies can—more is definitely not better where fertilizers are concerned.**

## Nitrogen-Deficiency Symptoms

**Tomatoes.** Plants grow slowly and the leaves are small, light greenish and/or yellowish. Top leaves may be light green with purple veins. Flower buds turn yellow and drop off. Fruits are often small.

**Corn.** Leaves are light green (instead of a nice dark green) or have yellowish center streaks, and growth is stunted. The lower leaves are usually affected first; they will gradually become dry and brown and fall off.

**Potatoes.** The leaves and stems turn light green or pale yellow. The young top leaves may curl upward and the plant itself is stunted. At harvesttime, the tubers will be small.

**Cucumbers.** Leaves turn yellow. Vines don't set very much fruit, and any fruit that is produced is light in color and pointy at the blossom end (the part farthest from the vine).

## Nitrogen Remedies

**Fast fix.** Scratch some alfalfa meal, composted animal manure, bloodmeal, or other high-nitrogen organic fertilizer into the surface of the soil around the plants. Or water the plants with a diluted solution of fish emulsion or spray it directly on the foliage. A warning here: If you add too much nitrogen, you'll get all plant and no fruit, especially with tomatoes. So be sure you don't overdo it.

**Long-term cure.** Growing and then turning under a nitrogen-fixing cover crop of clover, vetch, or peas is one of the best ways to add nitrogen to your garden (see "Putting On the Cover" on page 90 for details). Another good way to build up the nitrogen content of your beds is with generous supplies of compost, well-rotted manure, or other nitrogen-rich organic materials, preferably added in the fall.

*Yellow striping on leaves shows that these corn plants are nitrogen-deficient. The lower leaves are dying.*

## Phosphorus-Deficiency Symptoms

**Tomatoes.** Plants grow slowly. Leaves are dark green on top but have purple undersides. Seedlings grow very slowly.

**Corn.** Stalks are small and the leaves turn purple at the tips and along the margins.

**Potatoes.** Leaves and stems are somewhat stunted and darker green than normal. Leaves may curl upward. At harvesttime, there may be irregular brown specks inside your potatoes, many radiating outward from the core. (*Note:* Viruses and/or extreme temperatures can cause similar specks.)

## Phosphorus Remedies

**Fast fix.** Foliar feed with liquid bonemeal or work dry bonemeal or rock phosphate into the soil where roots can reach it. If you had this problem last year and haven't planted yet, add these materials to your planting holes and furrows as soon as possible.

*These stunted cornstalks aren't getting enough phosphorus. The purpling of the leaf tips is a clue to identifying this deficiency.*

**Long-term cure.** Low levels of organic matter and/or extremes of soil pH (too acid or alkaline) can worsen phosphorus deficiencies. Normally, earthworms, bacteria, and other soil-dwelling organisms will break down organic matter and release its plentiful supplies of phosphorus to the plants. But extremes of soil pH will limit the activity of these creatures and thus inhibit the availability of phosphorus. So test your soil's pH—it may have to be adjusted for any long-term remedy to be effective.

If your soil is too acid, work in some limestone; if it's too alkaline, add sulfur. Build up the organic matter content of your soil. You may also need to add some rock phosphate.

*The new leaves on this seedling seem healthy, but the yellow older leaves with brown edges are a symptom of potassium deficiency.*

## Potassium-Deficiency Symptoms

**Tomatoes.** Leaves become dark green, stems stay small, and leaves are bunched together (the leaves themselves may crinkle and curl upward). Older leaves become yellow, then brown at the edges. Fruits fall off the vine soon after ripening, have hard, blotchy flesh, and ripen unevenly.

**Corn.** Lower leaf tips and edges will become scorched and brown. Plants will grow slowly and have poorly developed root systems. Stalks will be weak, diseased, or both and often become so stressed that they snap off.

**Potatoes.** Growth is slow and plant growth is stunted. Leaves are very dark green in color. The leaves may turn brown at the edges and eventually die.

## Potassium Remedies

**Fast fix.** Scratch kelp meal or wood ashes into the soil around plants. With wood ashes, be sure to apply them only once every two or three years in any particular area to avoid creating soil imbalances.

**Long-term cure.** Build up potassium levels in your soil by adding some well-aged compost and/or composted manure. You can also enrich your garden beds with granite meal (a fine rock powder obtained from granite quarries)—it's a good source of slow-release potassium.

## Calcium-Deficiency Symptoms

**Tomatoes.** Blossom-end rot (the formation of a dry, brown spot on the part of the fruit opposite the stem). Tips of new shoots are stunted and distorted.

## Calcium Remedies

**Fast fix.** Water tomatoes evenly and regularly to allow calcium to reach the tomato flower at time of fruit formation.

**Long-term cure.** Add crushed eggshells (do you live close to a restaurant that serves breakfast?) to your compost or work crushed oyster shells or ground limestone into your garden beds—preferably in the fall or at least before planting.

*Blossom-end rot, caused by lack of calcium, is a sign of uneven soil moisture.*

## Magnesium-Deficiency Symptoms

**Tomatoes.** Older leaves turn yellow while the leaf veins stay dark green. Yellow areas eventually turn brown and die. Very few flowers and fruits form on the plant.

**Beans.** Older leaves turn yellow while the leaf veins stay dark green. Yellow areas eventually turn brown and die. Very few flowers and fruits form on the plant.

*Yellow areas on leaves between dark green veins are a classic symptom of lack of magnesium.*

### Magnesium Remedies

If your soil is also deficient in potassium, work Sul-Po-Mag (mined sulfate of potash-magnesia) into the root zone of the affected plants. If your soil is acidic (pH under 6), work in dolomitic lime to raise the pH and add magnesium at the same time.

### Iron-Deficiency Symptoms

**Tomatoes.** Youngest leaves turn yellow between the veins. Later, the whole leaf turns yellow, but older leaves remain green.

### Iron Remedies

**Fast fix.** Foliar feed with a liquid seaweed product.

**Long-term cure.** Alkaline soils that are poorly aerated or over-limed can be low in iron. Add sulfur to reduce soil alkalinity. If your soil is not alkaline, use iron sulfate.

*If the young leaves on your plants turn pale between the veins, but older leaves don't, the problem may be iron deficiency.*

## KEEP SOIL IN SHAPE WITH COVER CROPS

You can help keep your soil healthy and your plants happy by planting cover crops in your vegetable and annual flowerbeds. Cover crops are crops grown to protect and enrich the soil and to control weeds. You "harvest" organic matter and nutrients from cover crops by tilling the plants back into the soil. The optimum plan is to have a vigorous cover crop growing whenever you're not growing vegetables or flowers. In most areas in the United States, that means late fall through early spring, although in some southern areas, it may mean exactly the reverse—growing your cover during summer.

Here are eight great reasons to include cover crops in your garden plans:

**Cover crops provide nitrogen.** Nitrogen is what puts the green in your greens. It's also the plant food most likely to be deficient in sandy soil or any type of soil that's low in organic matter.

**Cover crops add organic matter.** As you now know, a high level of organic matter in soil provides nutrients, helps conserve water, and improves soil structure.

**Cover crops protect against erosion.** The top layer of your garden soil—the most fertile part—can slip away when assaulted by the winds and rain of winter. A cover crop holds it in place.

**Cover crops catch nutrients.** If your area gets heavy winter rains, important plant nutrients may literally be washed out of your soil. Plant a cover crop in the fall to take up these nutrients and release them back to the soil when you turn that crop under the following spring.

**Cover crops break up compacted soil.** Some cover crops, such as sweet clover and alfalfa, have thick, deep taproots, which can be very effective at breaking up hard soil.

**Cover crops control weeds.** Planting a vigorous cover crop such as vetches and crimson clover may well be the easiest way to beat troublesome weeds.

**Cover crops attract beneficials.** Many cover crops provide protection and food for beneficial insects that help control pests in your garden.

**quick tip**

How much cover crop seed should you sow? Seed for cover cropping is relatively cheap, so don't scrimp. A half-cup of most kinds of seed will cover about 100 square feet. To keep seed costs down, go together with a few other gardeners and buy a big bag of cover crop seed to share.

*Buckwheat makes a great garden fill-in to boost soil organic matter between spring and fall crops, and its flowers attract beneficial insects.*

## DON'T FORGET TO INOCULATE

SOME COVER CROPS are special plants called legumes (sweet clover and alfalfa are two examples). Legumes transform nitrogen from the air into nitrogen compounds that plants can use, with the help of bacteria called nitrogen-fixing bacteria. This helps you because it means you don't have to work as hard to add nitrogen to the soil.

These special bacteria may or may not be present in the soil already. There are many different strains, and the only way to ensure that the right strain is there when you plant a legume cover crop is to put it there yourself when you plant. To do so, you'll need to buy an inoculant, a commercially produced powder that contains the bacteria. All you have to do is coat the cover crop seed with inoculant and then plant. Once you've grown a particular kind of legume in your garden, the nitrogen-fixing bacteria it needs will persist in the soil for three to five years.

**Cover crops can be an effective mulch.** Grow vetch, rye, or a combination of the two in your garden, mow it or let it die back naturally (either by completing its life cycle or from winter cold) and you have a ready-to-go mulch that will retain moisture as it controls weeds. Till a narrow strip through it, or punch holes right into the mulch for your transplants.

### Putting On the Cover

Now that you're convinced of the advantages of growing a cover crop on your garden, here's how to go about it:

1. **Sow it.** Seeds left on top of the soil tend to dry out, wash away, or be eaten by birds. Covering the seed with a bit of soil gives it a much higher chance of success. A well-prepared seedbed is ideal, of course, but when that's not possible—if you want to sow a cover crop between established vegetable rows, for example—just rake the seed gently with a hand tool. This is especially important for large-seeded covers such as fava beans or cereal rye.

2. **Water it.** Give your garden a good soaking after planting a cover crop if there's no rain in the forecast. Another watering soon after the cover comes up will give it a competitive edge.

3. **Dig it.** What you do with your finished cover crop depends on what you plan to grow in your garden. If you've planted a legume cover to provide nitrogen for a crop such as tomatoes, turn the cover under about the time it flowers (that's when its nitrogen levels peak). Winter annual legumes typically flower between mid-April and late June.

   If the cover crop hasn't flowered, but you're ready to sow or transplant some vegetables, you can turn it under anyway. You can plant right after turning under a legume—unless it has added a lot of bulky material to your soil. (In this case, let it decompose and settle a bit.)

If your cover is not a legume, wait two to three weeks after you turn it under to plant. The decomposition of nonlegumes can tie up available nitrogen in the soil for a while.

And just *how* should you turn it under? That depends on how tall it is. The average "tiller" (either a machine with tines or a gardener with a turning fork) can easily handle a low-growing cover crop such as clover.

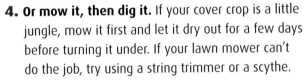

*If you plant a large area in cover crops, you'll need a roto-tiller or even a small tractor to turn it under. But for most home gardens, it's easy to dig in a cover crop by hand.*

**4. Or mow it, then dig it.** If your cover crop is a little jungle, mow it first and let it dry out for a few days before turning it under. If your lawn mower can't do the job, try using a string trimmer or a scythe.

Once the cover is cut, you can also consider setting aside the trimmings for use as a weed-smothering (and, with legumes, plant-fertilizing) mulch.

## How and When to Plant Cover Crops

**After summer crops.** Early flowers and vegetables such as sweet corn are generally finished producing by mid-August. If you don't intend to plant fall greens, clean up the bed and sow a cover crop by late August.

**Overseeded into standing crops.** If the vegetables or flowers in question will continue to produce until frost (or beyond), you can overseed the bed. Cast the seed into the standing crop in late summer as the weather starts to cool—remember, you want to have

In late summer, sow cover crop seed around crops like broccoli that will keep producing into the fall.

good growth before winter. Be sure that enough of it reaches bare ground to germinate and establish a cover. When you finally remove the spent crops, sow some more cover crop seed in this newly bare soil. You'll have a broader choice of cover crops—including more legumes—to choose from with earlier seeding.

**In the spring.** In areas with long, mild springs, sow a fast-growing cool-season cover such as a crimson clover, fava beans, or oats as soon as you can work the soil. To get your cover in earlier, you could even "frost seed": Just spread the seed on the bare, frozen ground and let the freezing-thawing heaving action of the warming soil "pull" the seed into the soil for you.

**Summer fallow.** If part of your garden is temporarily bare between spring and fall crops, put those long, warm summer days to good use with a quick-growing hot-weather green manure such as cowpeas, buckwheat, or HUBAM white sweet clover. You can even overseed while growing to extend your cover crop's time in the garden.

**Full-year green manure.** If you feel that your garden is getting a bit worn-out in spots, it may be time to give those hard-pressed areas a rest. A one-year cover crop will build up the soil's organic matter and nitrogen reserves, interrupt disease and pest

## quick tip

Cover crops offer your eye some much-needed green in the dull palette of winter, and their spring floral displays can be spectacular.

cycles, and give beneficial microorganisms, earthworms, and other helpful critters a boost. You can use perennials such as red clover and alfalfa or certain winter annuals such as crimson clover—if you remember to mow them before they flower. (If you mow after they flower, they'll die because they have completed their life cycle.)

**Living mulch.** Plant a low-growing perennial cover, such as white clover or a mixture of white clover and a low turfgrass, in early spring or late summer. At the proper time, turn under strips of this green growth with a hoe or tiller and direct-seed your vegetables or poke holes in it for transplants. This is not recommended for gardeners who face water restrictions because the living mulch needs a lot of extra moisture.

*Low-growing clover serves as a living mulch around broccoli and continues to protect the soil after the broccoli finishes producing.*

# Choose Your Cover Crop

Consult the listings below to decide which cover crop will work best for you. For example, fast-growing cover crops are good for filling beds between plantings of vegetable crops. Winter annuals serve well as a winter groundcover to prevent runoff. Check the "Comments" column for special hints on how to use each crop.

| SPECIES | TYPE | NORTHERN LIMIT (by USDA zone) | GROWTH RATE | SEEDING RATE (cups/100 sq. feet) | COMMENTS |
|---|---|---|---|---|---|
| **LEGUMES** | | | | | |
| Common/ white vetch (*Vicia sativa*) | WA | 7 | F | – | Flowers in early May in most regions |
| Purple vetch (*Vicia benghalensis*) | WA | 8 | F | – | Good winter-kill mulch in areas with hard frost |
| Red clover (*Trifolium pratense*) | SLP | 5 | M | ⅛–¼ | Not recommended for flooded soil; shade tolerant |
| White clover (*Trifolium repens*) | P | 5 | M | ⅛ | Low-growing; good living mulch; shade and drought tolerant |
| Crimson clover (*Trifolium incarnatum*) | WA | 6 | VF | ⅛–¼ | Reseeds itself; flowers mid-May in most zones; some shade tolerance |
| Berseem clover (*Trifolium alexandrinum*) | WA/ SA | 7 | VF | ⅛–¼ | Fast growth in cool and warm weather |
| Subterranean clover (*Trifolium subterraneum*) | WA | 7 | M | – | Reseeds by burrowing seed into ground; some drought tolerance |
| Fava beans (*Vicia faba*) | SA | 8 | F | 1 | Can also produce edible bean crop |
| Alfalfa (*Medicago sativa*) | P | 5 | S | ⅛ | Has deep taproot; won't grow in wet soils; low shade tolerance; high drought tolerance |
| Yellow-blossom sweet clover (*Melilotus officinalis*) | B | 5 | S | – | Has deep taproot; low shade tolerance; some drought tolerance |

| SPECIES | TYPE | NORTHERN LIMIT (by USDA zone) | GROWTH RATE | SEEDING RATE (cups/100 sq. feet) | COMMENTS |
|---|---|---|---|---|---|
| HUBAM white sweet clover (*Melilotus alba*) | SA | 8 | F | – | Rapid growth in warm weather; some drought tolerance |
| Cowpeas (*Vigna sinensis*) | SA | 10 | VF | – | Rapid growth in hot weather; prefers well-drained soil |
| **NONLEGUMES** | | | | | |
| Buckwheat (*Fagopyron esculentum*) | SA | 10 | VF | – | Good nutrient-catching and weed-smothering crop; low drought tolerance |
| Cereal/ winter rye (*Secale cereale*) | WA | 3 | VF | 1 | Can be planted later in fall than other covers; some drought and shade tolerance |
| Annual ryegrass (*Lolium multiflorum*) | WA | 4 | VF | – | May tie up nitrogen temporarily when turned under; shade tolerant; some drought tolerance |
| Oats (*Avena sativa*) | SA | 8 | VF | 1 | Very rapid growth in cool weather; low drought tolerance |

**KEY**

WA = Winter annual    SA = Summer annual    SLP = Short-lived perennial
P = Perennial    B = Biennial    S = Slow
M = Moderate    F = Fast    VF = Very fast

*Yellow-blossom sweet clover*

*Vetch*

# Your Seasonal Soil-Care Calendar

## JANUARY

Work out a three-year **rotation plan** for your vegetable garden. By changing the positions of plants in different plant families from year to year, you interrupt disease and pest cycles. Plan to **alternate deep-rooted plants** with shallow-rooted plants and heavy feeders with light feeders to avoid exhausting soil nutrients.

## FEBRUARY

**Order seeds** for your soil-building cover crops. Save money by buying a big bag of seed and splitting the cost—and the seed—with your gardening friends or neighbors.

## MARCH

Find a source for **compost**. Many counties and municipalities compost leaves and yard wastes for residents' use.

## APRIL

April showers bring May flowers. They also bring **erosion** and **drainage problems**. Take a walk in the rain and watch for places where the water runs off the soil surface. If it's causing soil erosion, try to figure out how you might be able to stop the runoff in the future (possibly by mulching or changing the surface grading). And when the rain stops, take a **soil sample** and have it tested by your local extension office.

- Don't be tempted to work the soil too early when it's still cold and wet.
- Begin **soil-building** activities. If spring cover crops (such as oats and clovers) are in your rotation plan, plant them now.
- If you planted a **cover crop** last fall, incorporate it as soon as you can work the soil. Get as much compost as you can carry home and dig it into your vegetable and flowerbeds.

- Low **soil temperatures** mean slow seed germination and plant growth in spring. Early planting won't save you time, and it may actually stunt the growth of your plants.
- Plant **spring vegetables** and—to give **summer crops** such as peppers, melons, and tomatoes an earlier start—lay black plastic over the planting bed for a couple of weeks to warm the soil.

## MAY

If you don't have a **compost bin**, build one. (Or just make a loose pile of compostable materials.) Then begin to fill it.

- Take corrective action based on your lawn and garden soil test results, using lime or sulfur to adjust pH and **organic fertilizers** to improve nutrient levels.
- Use straw or grass clippings to **mulch** around your vegetables.

**Winter**

**Spring**

**Summer**

**Fall**

# JUNE

Mulch your land-scaped areas. There are good reasons to wait until your soil warms, despite the fact that your neighbors applied mulch two months ago. Your plants will get a **healthier start** and you'll be giving desirable self-sowing **annual flowers** a chance to get going.

- As early **vegetable crops** go to seed, you can follow them with a **summer cover crop** (e.g., buckwheat, sudangrass, millet). Don't let these summer cover crops go to seed!

# JULY

Let the **decomposers** do the work this month—you've worked enough. Lend them a helping hand by turning the compost occasionally.

# AUGUST

As your vegetable crops mature, clean up the debris and plant a **fall cover crop** (for example, oats, crimson clover).

- **Cut down** your summer cover crops and turn them under the soil.

- Watch your compost steam (or turn it if it stops). Monitor its health by taking its temperature!

# SEPTEMBER

You can still **plant fall cover crops** (for example, annual rye, vetch, winter wheat, crimson clover).

- If you've experienced lawn or garden problems, have your **soil tested**.

# OCTOBER

Fertilize cool-season grasses and topdress your lawn with a thin layer of compost.

- If indicated on your soil test results, add lime or sulfur to adjust the pH of your soil.

- Top off your empty vegetable beds with raked-up grass clippings and **fall leaves**. Leaving soil bare exposes it to erosion and nutrient leaching.

- **Order some worms** and start an indoor worm composting bin for your kitchen scraps.

# NOVEMBER

Run over your **fallen leaves** with the lawn mower and either allow them to remain on your lawn or, if the leaf layer is too thick, drag them to your compost pile. You could also bag them to use as mulch next year.

# DECEMBER

**Feed the worms!** Remember to make use of your **Christmas greens** by laying them over your perennials. Pine needles or shredded leaves also make good materials for a winter mulch, which helps to insulate the soil and protect your plants from frost heaving.

# A Glossary of Soil Terms

Now that you've learned to "walk the walk" when it comes to caring for your soil, here are some terms to help you "talk the talk." You'll find many of these "earthy" words in this book as well as in materials pertaining to soil tests and test results.

**Aeration.** The exchange of air in the pore spaces of the soil with air in the atmosphere. Good aeration is necessary for healthy plant growth.

**Clay soil.** Soil that is made up of very fine particles that hold nutrients well but are poorly drained and difficult to work.

**Compaction.** Soil condition that occurs when there is heavy traffic over an area, causing pore spaces, which normally make up about half of the soil's bulk, to collapse.

**Compost.** Decomposed and partially decomposed organic matter that is dark in color and crumbly in texture. Used as an amendment, compost increases the water-holding capacity and drainage of the soil, and is an excellent nutrient source for microorganisms, which later release nutrients to your plants.

**Cover crop.** A crop grown to protect soil from erosion while also building organic matter and controlling weeds.

**Decomposers.** Organisms, usually soil bacteria, that derive nourishment by breaking down the remains or wastes of other living organisms into simple organic compounds.

**Double-digging.** A technique used to prepare a garden bed that entails first removing a layer of topsoil, loosening the subsoil, then replacing the topsoil mixing in organic matter in the process. This raises the soil surface and improves aeration in heavy soils.

**Earthworms.** Beneficial soil-dwelling worms that help to break down organic matter and, in the process, both loosen and aerate the soil.

**Fertilizer.** A natural or manufactured material added to the soil that supplies one or more of the major nutrients—nitrogen, phosphorus, and potassium—to growing plants.

**Foliar feeding.** A way to give grass a light nutrient boost by spraying plants with a liquid fertilizer that is absorbed through the leaf pores. Compost tea and seaweed extract are two examples of organic foliar fertilizers.

**Green manure.** A crop that, before it reaches full maturity, is incorporated into the soil for the purpose of soil improvement.

**Humus.** A dark-colored, stable form of organic matter that remains after most of the plant and animal residues in it have decomposed.

**Legume.** A plant that is a member of the pea family (including clover, alfalfa, beans, and peas), whose roots host nitrogen-fixing bacteria in a symbiotic relationship. By making atmospheric nitrogen available to plants, these bacteria improve the productivity of the soil.

**Loam.** The best texture of soil to have; it contains a balance of fine clay, medium-sized silt, and coarse sand particles. Loam is easily tilled and retains moisture and nutrients effectively.

**Micronutrient.** A nutrient plants need in very small quantities. Micronutrients include copper, chlorine, zinc, iron, manganese, boron, and molybdenum.

**Mulch.** A layer of an organic or inorganic material—such as shredded leaves, straw, bark, pine needles, lawn clippings or black plastic—that is spread around plants to conserve soil moisture and discourage weeds. As organic mulches decompose, they help to build the soil.

**NPK ratio.** The ratio of nitrogen (N), phosphorus (P), and potassium (K) in a fertilizer or amendment. For example, the NPK ratio for alfalfa meal is 5-1-2.

**Organic.** Materials that are derived directly from plants or animals. Organic gardening uses plant and animal by-products to maintain soil and plant health, and doesn't rely on synthetically made fertilizers, herbicides, or pesticides.

**pH.** A measure of how acid or alkaline a substance is. The pH scale ranges from 1 to 14, with 7 indicating neutrality, below 7 acidity, and above 7 alkalinity. The pH of your soil greatly affects what nutrients are available to your plants.

**Raised bed.** A garden bed raised above the soil surface to remedy poor drainage problems or to improve growing conditions. This can be done by double-digging the bed, or simply by loosening the top layer of soil and adding organic material.

**Rototiller.** A self-powered rotary tiller that pulverizes the soil with its rapidly turning blades. It is a useful tool for incorporating green manures and crop residues; however, overuse can damage the soil structure.

**Sandy soil.** Soil which contains more than 70 percent sand and less than 15 percent clay. Sandy soil is generally easy to work and well-drained, but it has poor nutrient- and water-holding abilities.

**Silt.** Refers to a soil particle of moderate size—larger than clay but not as large as sand.

**Soil amendment.** A material added to the soil for the purpose of making it more productive by improving its structure, drainage or aeration. An amendment such as compost can also be used to enhance microbial activity in the soil.

**Soil dwellers.** The living organisms that reside in the soil. These include decomposers such as bacteria, fungi and earthworms, beneficial parasites and predators, the larvae stages of many insects, and soil animals such as moles.

**Soil structure.** The physical arrangement of soil particles and interconnected pore spaces. Soil structure can be improved by the addition of organic matter. Walking on or tilling wet soil can destroy the soil aggregates and ruin the soil's structure.

**Soil test kit.** A set of instructions and a soil bag available through your state's Cooperative Extension Service. Test results indicate soil pH and specify what amendments and nutrients should be added to your soil to ensure success with your planned use.

**Soil texture.** The proportions of sand, silt and clay in a particular soil.

**Symbiotic relationship.** A mutually beneficial relationship between two living organisms, such as plant roots and nitrogen-fixing bacteria.

**Till.** To prepare the soil for planting seeds or to disturb it in order to control weeds, either with a power driven rototiller or with a hoe, spading fork or some other hand tool.

**Weeds.** Weeds are any plants that happen to grow where you don't want them to. Some perfectly fine plants can be considered weeds when they pop up in the wrong places.

# Recommended Reading & Resources

## Books & Periodicals

Carr, Anna, et al. *Rodale's Chemical-Free Yard & Garden*. Emmaus, PA: Rodale, 1991.

Gershuny, Grace. *Start with the Soil*. Emmaus, PA: Rodale, 1993.

Hynes, Erin. *Rodale's Successful Organic Gardening: Improving the Soil*. Emmaus, PA: Rodale, 1994.

Martin, Deborah L., and Grace Gershuny. *The Rodale Book of Composting*. Emmaus, PA: Rodale, 1992.

Ondra, Nancy J. *Soil and Composting: The Complete Guide to Building Healthy, Fertile Soil*. (Taylor's Weekend Gardening Guides.) Boston: Houghton Mifflin, 1998.

*Organic Gardening* magazine. Rodale, 33 East Minor Street, Emmaus, PA 18098.

Rodale, Maria. *Maria Rodale's Organic Gardening*. Emmaus, PA: Rodale, 1998.

## Tools, Supplies & Services

### A & L Agricultural Laboratories
7621 Whitepine Road
Richmond, VA 23237
Phone: (804) 743-9401
Fax: (804) 271-6446

### Bountiful Gardens
18001 Shafer Ranch Road
Willits, CA 95490-9626
Phone/fax: (707) 459-6410
Web site: www.zapcom.net/~bountiful

### Cape Cod Worm Farm
30 Center Avenue
Buzzards Bay, MA 02532
Phone: (508) 759-5664
Web site: members.aol.com/Capeworms/private/wormhome.htm

### Cook's Consulting
R.D. 2, Box 13
Lowville, NY 13367
Phone: (315) 376-3002
E-mail: pegcook@northnet.org

### Gardener's Supply Co.
128 Intervale Road
Burlington, VT 05401-2850
Phone: (800) 863-1700
Fax: (800) 551-6712
Web site: www.gardeners.com

### Happy D Worm Ranch Farm
1512 W. Whitendale Avenue
Visalia, CA 93277
Phone: (559) 738-9301
Fax: (559) 733-3250
Web site: www.happydranch.com

### Harmony Farm Supply and Nursery
3244 Gravenstein Hwy. North
Sebastopol, CA 95472
Phone: (707) 823-9125
Fax: (707) 823-1734
Web site: www.harmonyfarm.com

### Johnny's Selected Seeds
Foss Hill Road
Albion, ME 04910
Phone: (207) 437-4357
Fax: (800) 437-4290 (U.S. only)
Web site: www.johnnyseeds.com

Peaceful Valley Farm Supply
P.O. Box 2209
Grass Valley, CA 95945
Phone: (530) 272-4769
Fax: (530) 272-4794
Web site: www.groworganic.com

Woods End Research Laboratory, Inc.
P.O. Box 297
Mt. Vernon, ME 04352
Phone: (207) 293-2457
Fax: (207) 293-2488
Web site: www.woodsend.org

# Acknowledgments

Contributors to this book include Fern Marshall Bradley, Lynn Byczynski, Celia Cameron, Jill Jesiolowski Cebenko, Jeff Cox, Matt Damsker, Barbara Ellis, Mike Ferrara, Grace Gershuny (from *Start with the Soil*), Sarah Wolfgang Heffner, Carol Keogh, Cheryl Long, Deb Martin, Vicki Mattern, Mike McGrath, Scott Meyer, Pat Michalak, Diana Noble, Barbara Pleasant, Joanna Poncavage, Sally Roth, Pam Ruch, Marianne Sarrantonio, Delilah Smittle, and Catherine Yronwode.

## Photo Credits

**William Adams** 87 (top)

**Matthew Benson** v, 4, 5, 7, 15, 17, 18, 24, 36, 39, 40, 50, 53, 62, 70

**Rob Cardillo** 27, 28, 29, 42, 43, 45, 46, 47, 48, 51, 52, 65, 66, 74, 76, 77, 78, 81, 82, 89, 93, 95

**David Cavagnaro** 1

**Walter Chandoha** 23 (bottom left), 68, 80, 91

**E. R. Degginger/Bruce Coleman Stock** 13 (first on bottom left), 13 (bottom right),

**James F. Dill** 11 (second from top)

**Michael P. Gadomski/Bruce Coleman Stock** 13 (two small photos)

**G. M. Ghidiu** 11 (third from top)

**Ken Gracy Collection/Oregon State University** 13 (second from top)

**George H. Harrison/Grant Heilman Photography** 11 (top)

**Dency Kane** 22 (two bottom left), 23 (top left), 59, 67

**Mitch Mandel** 3, 8, 30 (top two), 31, 32, 35, 63

**Photodisc** 30 (bottom)

**Heath Robbins** 33

**Rodale Stock Images** 49

**Barry Runk/Grant Heilman Photography** 21

**Runk-Shoenberger/Grant Heilman Photography** 12, 22 (bottom right), 23 (right)

**Roger Sherman** 14

**J. B. Sieczka/Cornell University** 84, 85

**Ron Sutherland/Garden Picture Library** 19

**Michael S. Thompson** 54, 56, 57

**Ron West** 10, 11 (bottom), 13 (top), 13 (third from top), 86, 87 (bottom), 88

**Rick Wetherbee** 60

# Index

Dolomitic limestone, 41–42,
  47, 88
Double-digging, 72–75
Drainage
  diseases and, 16
  poor, working with, 19, *19*
  soil color and, 20
  testing, 17–18, *18*

# E

Earthworms, 14, *14,* 74, 85
Edging, 77–78, *78*
Eelworms, 12, *12*
Eggshells, 87
Elemental sulfur, 48
Erosion, controlling, 89

# F

Fertilizers, organic
  amount to use, 43
  vs. chemical, 3–4, *3*
  excessive use of, 41, 83
  feeding plants with, 7
  labels on, 41
  for nutrient deficiencies,
    83–88
  nutrient release from, *40*
  types, 45–48, *45, 46, 47, 48*
Fiery searchers, 10, *10*
Fireflies, 10, *10*
Fish emulsion, 84
Fish meal, 45, *45*
Flowerbeds, 75–78, *76, 77, 78*

# G

Glossary, 98–99
Gloves, 28, *28*
Goldenrod, *22*
Gooseneck hoes, 32
Granite meal, 87
Grass clippings
  leaving on lawn, 5
  as mulch, 50–51, *51, 53*
Green manures, 92–93
Greensand, 41, 47, *47*
Ground beetles, 10, *10*
Gypsum, 41, 48, *48*

# H

Hoes, 31–32, *31, 32*

# I

Insects
  beneficial, 2, 10–11, *10, 11,* 89
  harmful, 11–13, *11, 12, 13*
Iron, deficiency of, 88, *88*
Iron sulfate, 88

# J

Japanese beetles, 13, *13*
June beetles, 11, *11*

# K

Kelp meal, 86

# L

Lamb's-quarters, *23*
Lawns, 5, *5*
Leaves
  on lawn, 5
  as mulch, 52, *53*
  as soil amendment, 49, *49*
Legumes, 90–91
Lightning bugs, 10, *10*
Limestone
  misuse of, 4
  for nutrient deficiencies, 41, 86, 87
  raising pH with, 18–19, 41, 42, *42*
  types of, 47

# M

Magnesium
  deficiency of, 87–88, *87*
  described, 41
Magnesium limestone, 41–42, 47, 88
Manures
  green, 92–93
  as mulch, 52
  for nutrient deficiencies, 41, 84, 86
  as soil amendment, 49
Mattocks, 31, *31*
May beetles, 11, *11*
Micronutrients, 42

Milky disease spores, as pest control, 13
Millipedes, 11, *11*
Moisture, checking soil for, 75, *76*
Mounding, raised beds, 80
Mulch
    compost as, 63–64
    cover crops as, 90, 91
    living, 93, *93*
    materials for, 50–52, *50, 51,* **53**
    need for, *36*
    using, 77, *77*
Mullein, *23*
Mushroom compost, 68

# N

Nematodes, 12, *12*
Newspaper
    as mulch, 50, 52, *52, 53*
    preparing beds with, 79, 81, *81*
Nitrogen
    from cover crops, 89
    deficiency of, 84–85, *84*
    excessive use of, 41
    fertilizers, 45, *45*
    testing for, 40
Nutrient deficiencies
    calcium, 87, *87*
    diagnosing, 83
    iron, 88, *88*
    magnesium, 87–88, *87*
    nitrogen, 84–85, *84*
    phosphorus, 85–86, *85*
    potassium, 86–87, *86*
Nutrients
    excessive use of, 41, 83
    testing for, 39–41

# O

Onion hoes, 32
*Organic Gardening* magazine, 62
Oyster shells, 87

# P

Peas, 84–85
Peat moss, 6, 49
Perennials, beds for, 75–78, *76, 77, 78*

pH
    adjusting, 41–43
    levels, 42–43, **43**
    testing, 18–19, 21
Phosphorus
    deficiency of, 85–86, *85*
    described, 40
    fertilizers, 46, *46*
Pickaxes, 31, *31*
Pine needles, as mulch, 51–52
Pitchforks, 29
Plants, feeding, 7
Potash magnesia, sulfate of, 47–48, *47,* 88
Potassium
    deficiency of, 86–87, *86*
    described, 40–41
    fertilizers, 46–47, *47, 48*
Potatoes
    nitrogen-deficient, 84
    phosphorus-deficient, 85, *85*
    potassium-deficient, 86
Potted plants, 79
Power tools, 25

# R

Raised beds, preparing, 79–81, *80, 81*
Rakes, 30, *30*
Ribbon test, 16, **16**
Rock phosphate
    described, 46, *46*
    using, 40, 85, 86

# S

Salad burnet, *23*
Seasonal care calendar, 96–97
Seaweed, 41, 88
Seedlings, *ii*
Shovels, 27, *27*
Soil
    building healthy, 6–7, *7, 36*
    components of, 1–2, *2, 8,* 9–10
    vs. dirt, 2
Soil amendments. *See also* Beds, preparing;
    *specific amendments*
    types, 48–49, *49*
    using, 3–4, 6, *36, 77*
Soil samples, collecting, 38–39, *39, 77*

# USDA Plant Hardiness Zone Map

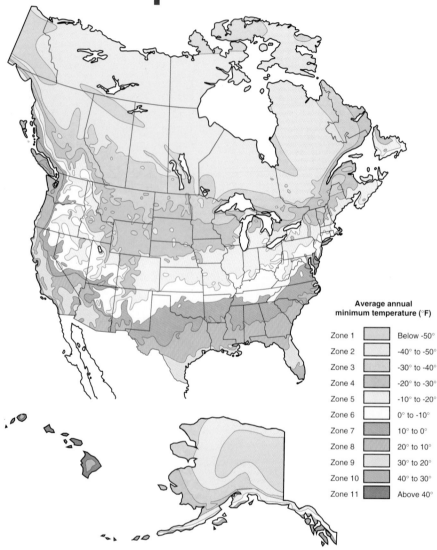

**Average annual minimum temperature (°F)**

|  | |  |
|------|---|-------------|
| Zone 1 | | Below -50° |
| Zone 2 | | -40° to -50° |
| Zone 3 | | -30° to -40° |
| Zone 4 | | -20° to -30° |
| Zone 5 | | -10° to -20° |
| Zone 6 | | 0° to -10° |
| Zone 7 | | 10° to 0° |
| Zone 8 | | 20° to 10° |
| Zone 9 | | 30° to 20° |
| Zone 10 | | 40° to 30° |
| Zone 11 | | Above 40° |

This map was revised in 1990 and is recognized as the best indicator of minimum temperatures available. Look at the map to find your area, then match its color to the key at the right. When you've found your color, the key will tell you what hardiness zone you live in. Remember that the map is a general guide; your particular conditions may vary.